RICK STEIN
FISH
&SHELLFISH

BBC
BOOKS

10 9 8 7 6

Rick Stein's Seafood first published in 2001.
This fully revised and updated edition,
first published in 2014 by BBC Books,
an imprint of Ebury Publishing
A Random House Group Company

The Random House Group Limited
Reg. No. 954009

Penguin Random House is committed to a
sustainable future for our business, our readers
and our planet. This book is made from Forest
Stewardship Council® certified paper.

FSC
www.fsc.org

MIX
Paper from
responsible sources
FSC® C018179

Addresses for companies within the
Random House Group can be found
at www.randomhouse.co.uk

A CIP catalogue record for this book
is available from the British Library

ISBN: 978 1 849 90845 0

Editor: Mari Roberts
Design and art direction: Smith & Gilmour
Photographer: James Murphy
Food stylist: Aya Nishimura
Assistant food stylist: Xenia von Oswald
Prop stylist: Penny Markham
Illustration: 1 Patrick Knowles; 340–7 Charlotte Knox

Colour origination by AltaImage, London
Printed and bound by Firmengruppe APPL,
aprinta druck, Wemding, Germany

To buy books by your favourite authors and
register for offers visit www.randomhouse.co.uk

CONTENTS

INTRODUCTION

Fourteen years ago the Padstow Seafood School opened. I don't know if it was the view out over the estuary across the water to Rock, the blue and white fish tiles, the warm wooden floor or the sail-shaped ceiling, but it was instantly successful. Maybe it was the quality of the fish and shellfish we used. I came to see that many people just didn't realize how good fresh fish could be. To help the students, I decided to write a book telling them everything they needed to know about fish and shellfish, and called the book *Seafood*. Like the school, it was also very popular.

Since that time, quite a lot has changed in my seafood world; in the techniques and styles of dishes and even the fish we use now. We're about to celebrate the Seafood Restaurant's fortieth birthday, so there are plenty of reasons to revise the original book with new recipes and, at the same time, take a nostalgic look back over many of the dishes we've cooked at the restaurant, such as Dover sole à la meunière. I still dust the firm-textured fish with flour, shake off the excess and give it a final slap on both sides to achieve the lightest of coatings; I still mention the idea behind the word 'meunière', of the fish being turned over in the floury hands of the miller's wife before being fried, but even in this simple technique I've made a change. Now I season the fish with salt; originally I put the salt in with the flour and it was never seasoned enough. In fact, every recipe in this book that was in the original book has been changed in some small way to reflect forty years' experience.

I've picked up lots of new ideas, too, such as cooking fish 'a la plancha', which comes from my cookery series in Spain. Translated it means 'on the griddle' but that barely sums up the theatre of a Spanish chef throwing a little olive oil on to a jumping hot, shiny steel plate then tossing a fillet of fish, skin-side down, on to it to achieve a beautifully crisp skin, turning it over and perhaps adding a ladle of slowly cooked garlic, then scooping the whole lot on to a plate. I've also learnt how to cook fish at the lowest of temperatures, fish such as salmon and tuna, by putting them into a sealed plastic bag immersed in a water bath brought up to no more than 50°C, then served so that it looks raw but cuts like butter. From a trip to Japan, I learnt much more of the techniques of sashimi making. There are new recipes based on fourteen years' more experience in Padstow, but also dishes brought back from filming in France, the Mediterranean, Spain, South-east Asia and India, as well as from my restaurant Bannisters at Mollymook in Australia. I've been to lots of other seafood restaurants in that time too and picked up, paradoxically, a lot of very uncheffy – but to me much more appetizing – ways of cooking and presenting food.

The overriding principle behind all the recipes in this book is: 'Would I cook this at home?' I've pared down all the recipes, and taken a view that most people will have a kitchen with equipment to make the job a lot easier, for example, a deep-fat fryer or a wok-shaped pan or a food processor or even a temperature probe, which you can now get for about £10. In the early days I'd describe how to deep-fry by testing the oil temperature with a piece of bread. I don't want to have to write that every time fish is fried any more. The recipes are also designed to use bought-in products such as mayonnaise or chilli sauce. Fourteen years ago it would have been unthinkable, everything had to be home-made; now I'm happy to enthuse about a product such as Kewpie mayonnaise. It's almost like a smart version of salad cream, and with fried grilled fish and a dollop of chilli relish I'm taken back to Ginza in Tokyo, sitting on beer crates with a table top resting on more crates, eating crisp fish with Kewpie's and drinking far too many Sapporos. I've done the same with harissa; I've given my own recipe but suggested what to buy if you don't want to make your own.

I've also simplified the grouping of fish for cooking. I realized that most species of fish can be cooked in the same way whether in the northern or southern hemispheres. There are only a couple of rules: oily fish doesn't suit rich sauces; you can't put delicate fish on a barbecue, or expect it not to fall apart in a fish stew. That's about it. Fish with a medium-oil content such as bass, snapper, mullet, grouper can be used for virtually any fish dish.

I have, however, gone to town with suggesting alternative fish for each recipe. This is partly because I know a lot more about fish in all the countries where this book might be available, but also because we've all gone through something of a sea change in our attitude to fish and shellfish because of the need to conserve fish stocks. Many of the alternatives I've suggested are from healthy stocks, but also the mere fact of pointing out other fish takes the pressure off popular species like cod, plaice, snapper or bass.

It's been a challenge to run fish restaurants with a menu that sticks only to species from healthy stocks. The Marine Conservation Society in Britain and other similar organizations elsewhere have come up with a Good Fish Guide, where all common species are rated like traffic lights. Green for go, amber for caution, while red simply means don't buy.

We've been able to stop selling fish on the red list, such as shark, North Atlantic halibut, ray and eels, but it's almost impossible to produce attractive menus with just green-rated fish. We have a policy at the Seafood Restaurant to sell only wild fish, so we've had to encroach on the amber list but, thanks to fish farming, sustainable fish cookery at home is easier. There are still problems with fish farming, though, such as the feed, which is mostly other smaller fish, and the need for chemicals to control diseases and parasites in dense populations, but I've always felt that, like good farming practice, good fish farming husbandry will prevail.

It's been lots of fun doing this book. Fish is still my first love, and looking back over the first forty years of the Seafood Restaurant I still feel the same as I did then: there's nothing more exhilarating than fresh fish simply cooked.

BUYING FISH

My recipes, being very straightforward, require truly fresh fish to make them shine. Buying the freshest fish is therefore essential. I worry that my recipes will not work as well if people only have the average fish counter at a supermarket to rely on. But even faced with a limited selection of fish, there's always going to be something good to buy. The cardinal rule is to be flexible. Large John Dory, for example, can be used instead of brill or turbot; monkfish dishes can be made with swordfish or John Dory. Choose the best-looking fish on the counter and go for that. Look for the brightest eye, the most sparkling skin. Like wine tasting, it's easier to make a judgement of quality by contrasting one fish with another.

Look for the following signs of quality:
EYES – clear and bright, not cloudy and sunken or blotched with red.
SKIN – shiny and vivid. Colours such as orange spots on plaice, the green and yellow flecks on cod and the turquoise, green and blue lines on mackerel should be bright and cheerful. Slime on fish is a good sign.
FINS – clearly defined and perky, not scraggy and broken.
GILLS – startling lustrous pink or red, moist and a delight to the eye, not faded or brown.
SMELL – fresh fish doesn't smell of fish, just of the sea. It should be appetizing; something you want to eat, not something the odour of which you hope will disappear when you cook it. It won't.
FEEL – firm. Obviously some fish is softer than others, but all fish goes slack and feels flabby as it goes stale.

FARMED FISH
Farmed fish have one advantage over wild: freshness can be perfectly controlled, because the fish are kept alive until they are ordered. Otherwise the quality is not quite as good as that of wild, mainly because the fish tend to be sold when they are too small and the flavour has not had a chance to develop. There are signs, however, that fish may be allowed to mature in the future. I have recently bought farmed turbot weighing over 3kg and the flavour was excellent. Salmon, too, are harvested in larger sizes.

There is a big difference between organic fish from low-density pens and cheap fish from over-populated tanks. If you can select your cut from a whole fish you will notice that the top-quality fish are much sleeker and firmer than the cheaper ones, which are stubby and quite often have truncated fins – an indication of overcrowding in the pens. When buying prepared fillets of salmon, look for firm flesh and leave the flabby stuff alone.

FILLETED FISH
It's harder to tell the freshness of fish fillets because there are fewer indicators to go by. But, as with whole fish, fillets should look bright and shiny. The flesh should be white, pink or off-white depending on the species. Fillets that are going stale will have a yellow – or worse – a brown tinge about them. Fresh fillets should be firm to the touch and should not smell. A simple rule I follow when buying fillets is to ask myself if I would like to eat them raw, sliced and served as the Japanese dish sashimi, with wasabi and soy.

STORING FISH
Domestic fridges are not ideal for storing fish; they are set at about 5°C and fish should be stored at 0°C if possible. Ideally, cook the fish the day you buy it. If you have to store it for a short time, keep it covered in the coldest part of the fridge.

DEFROSTING FROZEN FISH AND SHELLFISH

The quicker you defrost frozen food, the better the quality. Ice conducts heat faster than water so food freezes much more quickly than it thaws, and the longer you take to thaw, the more the ice in the centre can damage the structure by thawing, then refreezing a little, then thawing again. It's difficult to judge the cooking temperature at the centre of a piece of fish if you cook it from frozen. Best to defrost in the kitchen, not in the fridge.

BUYING CRUSTACEANS

Lobsters and crabs are sold either live or cooked. They are never sold dead and uncooked because the flesh deteriorates quickly and becomes mushy and tasteless. Cooking stops this process. Live lobsters or crabs should be obviously alive, with clear signs of muscular activity, whether aggressive waving of the claws in crabs or snapping of the tail in lobsters. Claws, tails and legs should not be dangling limply.

Whether cooked or raw, crustaceans should feel heavy for their size as this is an indication of good muscle quality. Compare the weights of two similarly sized lobsters or crabs by weighing them in each hand; opt for the heavier as it will have more meat. It's hard to get consistent quality in cooked lobsters and crabs because you are dependent on your fishmonger as the cook. How much salt, if any, did they use? How long did they cook the crustaceans for? What was the quality like before cooking? It's really a question of sticking to a fishmonger you know and trust.

PRAWNS

Prawns are sold either raw or cooked and can be bought whole with their heads still on or as tails, which can be either peeled or unpeeled. Prawn tails are better value for money than whole prawns, but whole prawns are usually better quality. The shells preserve the flavour and, once removed, can be used to make stocks and flavoured oils.

Prawns are normally sorted by size and sold by the average number per kg. If the fishmonger is offering 20–25 prawns per kg, the prawns will be large enough for most purposes. The lower the number of prawns per kg, the bigger the prawns and the more expensive they will be.

With the exception of local catch, the majority of prawns available will be frozen. 'Fresh' prawns will almost always have been frozen and then defrosted at their destination. Prawns freeze well, but do not travel well chilled, which is why they are usually boiled at sea if they are not to be frozen. Like lobsters, prawns deteriorate after death and become soft and tasteless very quickly. Unless they are local, or I can get them still alive, I always prefer to buy frozen raw prawns of the best quality.

Once the prawns are defrosted, again they deteriorate quickly. So, when buying 'fresh', make sure the prawns feel firm, that the shells are taut, intact and not dull looking. Make sure too that they smell fresh – definitely not of ammonia – and avoid any that have signs of darkening or black spots around the head.

DUBLIN BAY PRAWNS

These prawns, also known as langoustines or scampi, are more like lobsters, and care should be taken if buying them raw as, like raw prawns, they deteriorate rapidly. When buying cooked langoustines, give the tails a flick; there should be some spring left in them, indicating the muscle was in good condition when the prawn was cooked.

BUYING LIVE SHELLFISH

All uncooked shellfish, whether living in two shells (bivalves) or one (univalves), should be alive before cooking. The shells of bivalves, such as oysters, cockles, mussels and clams, should be closed or should close when tapped or squeezed together. Broken shellfish and those that don't close should be discarded. It's advisable not to buy from a batch where many of the shells are open because it's a sign that they have been out of the sea too long and won't taste fresh.

If the shells of mussels, cockles or clams don't open after cooking, it's *not* a sign that they are dead, so don't discard them: prise them open and eat them.

You can tell if univalves, such as whelks, winkles and abalone, are alive if you can see the creature moving inside the shell, if the shell moves, or if there is foam on the opening of the shell.

Live shellfish that you buy from a fishmonger will have health certification. If you are gathering your own, be aware that they can present a health risk if taken from a polluted area. Shellfish taken from the seashore are safer than those found in estuaries and harbours because any pollution is likely to be diluted by the open sea. Whenever gathering your own shellfish, it is advisable to ask for advice locally.

CLEANING AND STORING SHELLFISH

Wash shellfish in cold water to remove sand and mud, and scrape away any barnacles or weed. With mussels, remove the threads that attach the mussel to the rocks just before cooking. They don't keep well once this has been removed. Shellfish can be stored for a few days in the bottom of a fridge covered with seaweed or a damp cloth. Disregard any information about cleansing them in buckets of water with oatmeal or flour – they will not purge themselves because there will be no oxygen in the water and so they won't open.

EQUIPMENT & INGREDIENTS

Knives. A large cook's knife with a 25cm blade for chopping and cutting lobsters in half. A thin-bladed, flexible filleting knife that will allow you to feel both the fillet and bones. A small-bladed 7.5cm knife for opening raw clams, etc. A very sharp, long-bladed knife for thinly slicing salmon, smoked salmon or tuna.

Fish kettle. For poaching whole fish such as salmon, sea bass and coral trout. It can also double up as a steamer and as a water bath for very gentle cooking of fish in a bag.

Deep-fat fryer. These are thermostatically controlled, so safer to use than ordinary pans. Essential for fish cookery.

Fish-scaler. You can use a knife, or even a scallop shell, but this makes the job easier.

Fish slice. I like the very thin stainless steel ones, with a wide splay to lift fish easily and more slots than steel so that cooking oil drips off quickly.

Conical strainer, ladle and fine sieve. For straining soups and stocks.

Kitchen scissors. For cutting off fins.

Fish pliers or tweezers. For pin-boning.

Winkle pickers (very fine, short skewers or long pins). For removing winkles and whelks from the shell.

Lobster crackers and lobster pick.

Large, heavy-based, non-stick frying pan.

Petal steamer. For steaming fish and vegetables.

Fish clamp. For barbecuing.

Pair of long-handled tongs.

Cleaver and mallet. For portioning whole fish such as large cod, blue-eye trevalla or turbot.

Cast-iron or steel griddle. For cooking a la plancha.

Wok or deep chef's pan. The pan I use most.

Large shallow pan with a well-fitting lid. For steaming and braising.

Temperature probe.

Large roasting tin. For baking whole fish.

Food processor. For making light work of soups, mayonnaise, purées and pastes.

Cheap wooden chopsticks and a sushi mat. For home-smoking fish.

Very large saucepan. For cooking crabs, lobsters and langoustines.

Spice grinder.

And finally – if you love gadgets, as I do, a **smoke gun** to make home-smoking very easy.

HANDY STORE-CUPBOARD INGREDIENTS

Anchovies: good quality fillets in olive oil

Black beans: Chinese salted, fermented

Bonito flakes

Capers

Coatings for pan-frying fish: semolina, couscous, dried breadcrumbs such as panko

Dashi granules

Fennel herb: best grow it yourself, it's hard to buy

Fish sauce, such as Thai nam pla

Fresh ginger root

Ketjap manis (Indonesian soy sauce)

Olive oil: a well-flavoured extra virgin

Olives: good-quality, whole

Nam prik (sweet chilli and dried shrimp sauce)

Pernod or Ricard

Porcini, dried

Rice noodles, dried, of various kinds

Saffron

Sea salt flakes

Seaweed, Japanese: kombu and nori

Soy sauce: light, dark and tamari (soy sauce with less wheat and more soy beans)

Spices: cardamom, cayenne pepper, chilli flakes (crushed, dried), chipotle chillies, cinnamon, cloves, coriander seeds, cumin seeds, fennel seeds, fenugreek, mustard seeds (black and yellow), nutmeg, paprika, peppercorns (black and white), sichuan peppercorns, star anise, turmeric powder

Sun-dried tomatoes in olive oil

Tamarind: a block of pulp

Vermouth, dry white, such as Noilly Prat

Vinegar: sherry, red, white and balsamic

XO Sauce (Chinese preparation made with dried seafood and chilli)

TECHNIQUES

Scaling and gutting small round fish

See recipe on page 163.

1. Work under cold running water or over several sheets of newspaper. Grip the fish by its tail and scrape it from the tail towards the head, working against the direction in which the scales lie, using a fish-scaler or the blade of a blunt, thick-bladed knife.

2. Cut away the dorsal, pelvic and anal fins using a strong pair of kitchen scissors.

3. Slit open the belly of the fish from the anal fin up to the head and pull out the guts.

4. Cut away any remaining pieces of gut left behind in the cavity with a small knife and then wash it out with plenty of cold water.

5. To barbecue or grill the fish, slash the flesh 4 or 5 times down each side. Rub it with oil and season with a little salt and pepper.

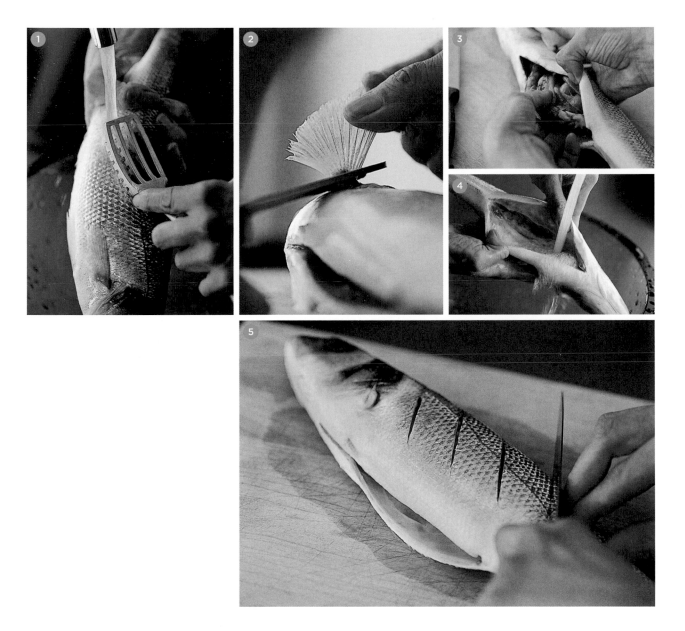

Preparing small oily fish for grilling

See recipe on page 210.

1. Rub off the scales with your thumb, then rinse the fish under cold running water.

2. Cut off the head and discard. If you want to remove the guts without slitting the fish open, give the belly a gentle squeeze. Trap the exposed guts under the blade of a knife and drag them out.

3. Alternatively, slit the fish open along the belly, all the way down to the tail, and pull out the guts with your hand. Wash the cavity clean.

4. Open up the gut cavity and put the fish belly-side down on a chopping board. Start to press down firmly along the backbone with the palm of your hand.

5. Continue pressing firmly all along the backbone until the fish is completely flat.

6. Turn the fish over and pull away the backbone, snipping it off at the tail end with scissors. Remove any small bones left behind in the fillet with fish pliers or tweezers. Season inside and out and then push back into shape. Grill the fish under a high heat for 2 minutes on each side.

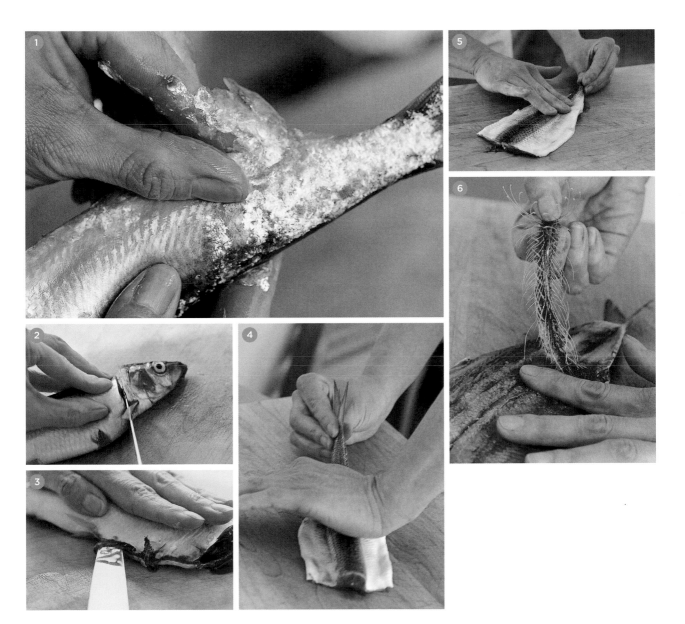

Filleting small round fish

1. With the back of the fish facing you, make a cut behind the back of the head, down to the backbone, using a sharp, thin-bladed, flexible knife.

2. With the knife still in place, turn it towards the tail and start to cut away the fillet. As soon as the whole blade of the knife is underneath the fillet, put your other hand flat on top of the fish and cut it away in one clean sweep, keeping the knife as close to the bones and as flat as possible.

3. Lift off the fillet, turn the fish over and repeat the process.

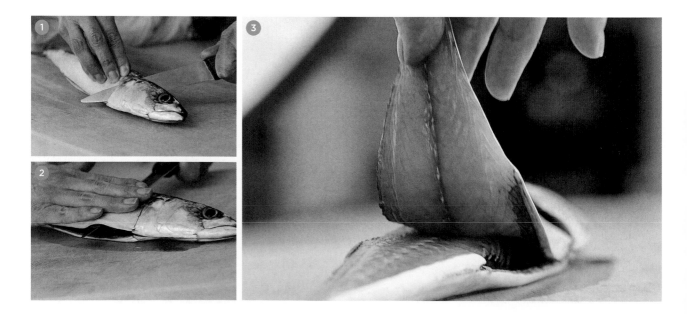

Filleting small round fish for stuffing

See recipe on page 221.

1. Remove the head of the fish. Start to cut away the top fillet until you can get the whole blade of the knife underneath it (see opposite, steps 1 and 2). Rest your other hand on top of the fish and cut the fillet away from the bones until you are about 2cm away from the tail.

2. Turn the fish over and repeat on the other side.

3. Pull back the top fillet and snip out the backbone close to the tail with scissors. The fillets will still be attached by the tail.

4. Spread the cut face of one fillet with your chosen paste, then put the fish back into shape.

5. Tie the fish in two places with string. Grill or barbecue for 3 minutes on each side.

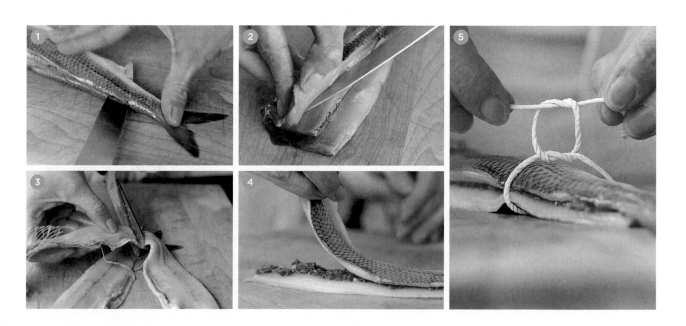

Filleting a large round fish

See recipe on page 131.

1. Scale the fish (see page 16) and then remove the head by cutting diagonally just behind the gills on both sides from under the pelvic fin around to the top of the head. This will retain all the fillet.

2. Starting at the head end, cut through the skin slightly to one side of the backbone along the whole length of the fish, using a sharp, thin-bladed, flexible knife.

3. Return to the head end and gradually cut the fillet away from the bones, keeping the blade as close to the bones as you can. When you reach the ribcage, if the bones are thick, continue to cut close to them until the fillet comes free. However, if the bones are fine, cut through them and remove them from the fillet with fish pliers or tweezers afterwards.

4. As you near the tail end, get the whole blade of the knife under the fillet, rest the other hand on top of the fish and cut the remainder away in one clean sweep. Turn the fish over and repeat on the other side.

5. Remove any bones from the fillets with fish pliers or tweezers.

6. Trim up the edges of each fillet and cut away the thinnest part of the belly flap. Cut the fillet across into portion-sized pieces weighing around 200g.

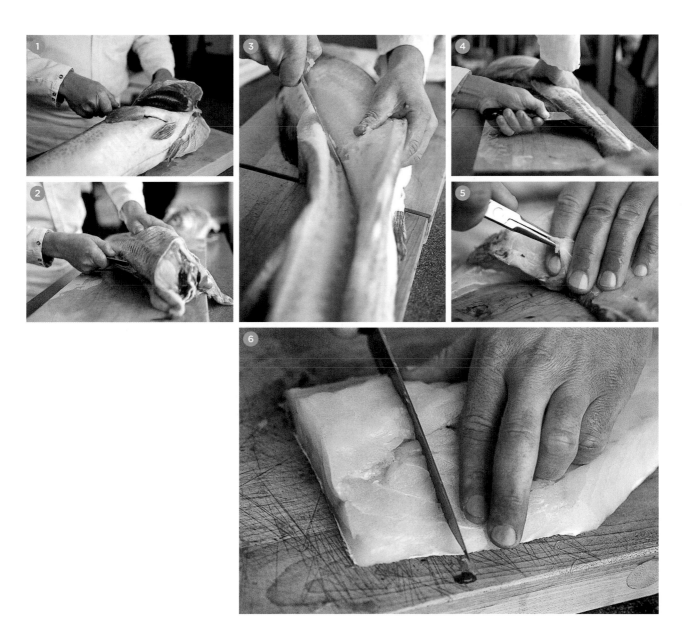

Preparing and griddling elongated fish

See recipe on page 223.

1. Don't bother to gut small fish. Cut around the back of the head with a sharp, thin-bladed, flexible knife.

2. With the knife still in place, turn it towards the tail and start to cut away the fillet, keeping the blade as flat against the bones as you can. As soon as the whole blade of the knife is under the fillet, rest your other hand on top of the fish and cut the fillet away in one clean sweep, down towards the tail. Turn the fish over and repeat on the other side.

3. Brush some marinade over both sides of each fillet and leave for 5 minutes to allow the flavours to permeate the fish a little. Heat a flat or ridged cast-iron griddle until smoking hot. Add the fillets and cook them for 1–1½ minutes on each side. Transfer them to a plate to stop them cooking any further.

Preparing monkfish

See recipe on page 181.

1. First remove the skin from the monkfish tail. Put the tail belly-side down on a board. Release and pull back some of the skin at the wider end of the tail so that you can get a sharp, flexible-bladed knife underneath to cut through the fine dorsal spines.

2. Grab hold of the wider end of the tail in one hand and the skin in the other and briskly pull it away, down over the tail.

3. Remove the two fillets by cutting along either side of the thick backbone with a sharp, thin-bladed, flexible knife, keeping the blade as close to the bone as you can.

4. Pull off the thin membrane that encases the fillets, releasing it with the knife where necessary.

5. Cut the fillets across into thin slices for ceviche (see page 181) or use according to your recipe.

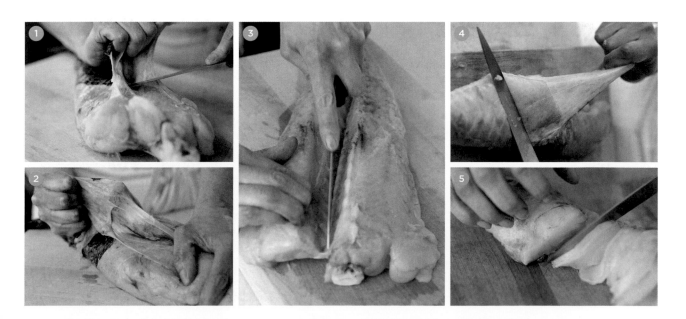

Filleting a sea bream and similar round fish

See recipe on page 170.

1. Remove the scales using a knife or fish-scaler, working from the tail to the head against the lie of the scales. Work in a sink to minimize scales flying everywhere.

2. Slit the belly open from the anal fin to the head and remove the guts.

3. Separate the fillets from the head by cutting round the fish just behind the gills down to the bone. Remove each fillet by cutting through the skin slightly to one side of the backbone along the whole length of the fish. Use a thin-bladed, flexible knife cutting in sweeps rather than sawing.

4. Keeping the knife as close to the bones as possible, gradually cut the fillet away, lifting it up as you do so. When you come to the ribcage, cut through the rib bones and lift the fillet off.

5. Slide the knife under the rib bones and remove them.

6. With your fingertip, find the row of pin bones running down the middle of each fillet and remove with tweezers or a small pair of fish pliers. They run a third of the way down the fillet and are not joined to any other bones.

7. The fillet is now ready for cooking according to your recipe.

8. Don't throw away the head and bones. Use for making the fish stock on page 310, and freeze if not wanted immediately.

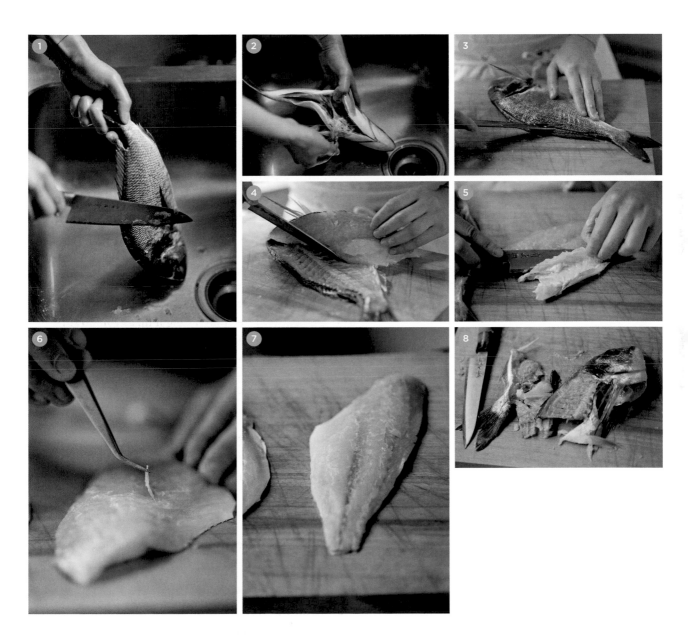

A special technique for preparing gurnard

See recipe on page 159.

1. Place the fish belly-side down on a chopping board. Make a shallow vertical cut just behind the head of the gurnard, where the spines of the dorsal fin begin.

2. Turn the blade of the knife horizontally towards the tail and take the dorsal fin in the other hand.

3. Slice just under the skin through the bones of the dorsal fin, right the way along the entire length of the fish, and lift them away.

4. Cut through the backbone where it joins the back of the head but not right the way through the fish.

5. Push your thumbs underneath the skin on either side of the head and pull it away slightly.

6. Take hold of the head in one hand and the body of the fish in the other, and pull the head down towards the belly.

7. As soon as the head becomes free, use it to help pull away the skin from the body of the fish.

8. Pull the skin off the whole fish and right over the tail. The fish is now ready for pan-frying.

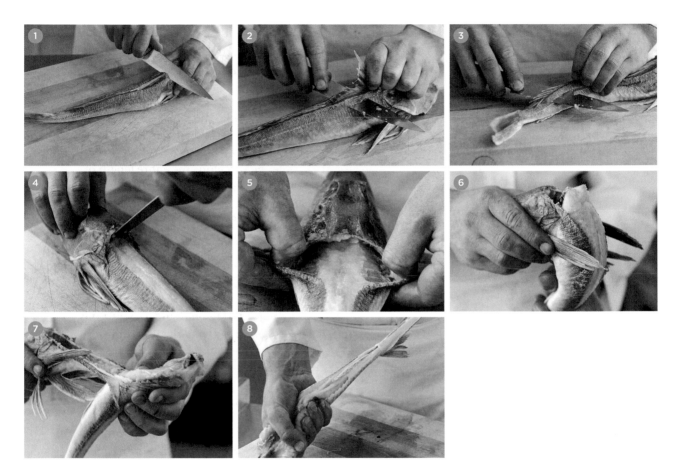

Preparing whiting for deep-frying whole

See recipe on page 148.

1. Scale, gut and trim the whiting. Twist the fish into a circle so that the tail goes into its mouth.

2. Push a cocktail stick up through the soft part of its under-mouth, through the tail and out through the top of the head. Season the fish inside and out with salt and pepper.

3. Coat the fish well on all sides in seasoned flour, then knock off the excess.

4. Dip the floured fish in beaten egg, making sure that it is well covered.

5. Finally, coat the fish in fresh white breadcrumbs, pressing them on well to make sure that it gets well covered with a thick, even coating. The fish is ready for deep-frying.

Preparing flatfish for grilling

See recipe on page 237.

1. Remove the lateral bones that run through the frills and part way into the flesh of the fish by cutting very close to the underlying fillet with scissors.

2. This will remove the frills and about 1cm of the adjacent flesh, which is full of little bones.

3. Score the fish on both sides like the veins of a leaf using a sharp knife. Marinate according to the recipe (see, for example, page 237), then grill the fish, dark-side up, under a high heat for 7–8 minutes.

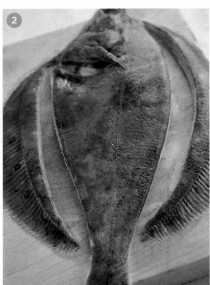

Preparing flatfish for deep-frying

See recipe on page 242.

1. To fillet the fish, cut around the back of the head, down to the backbone, using a sharp, thin-bladed, flexible knife. Then make a cut down the centre of the fish, from head to tail.

2. Starting at the head, slide the knife under one fillet and carefully cut it away, keeping the blade as flat and as close to the bones as possible. Remove the adjacent fillet, then turn the fish over and repeat.

3. Lay the fillet skin-side down, with the narrowest end facing you. Hold the tip of the skin with your fingers and, angling the blade of the knife down towards the skin and working it away from you, start to cut between the flesh and the skin. Firmly take hold of the skin and continue to work away from you, sawing the knife from side to side, keeping the blade close against the skin until the fillet is released.

4. Trim the frills away from the edge of the skinless fillet to give it a neat finish.

5. Slice the fillets diagonally into goujons about the thickness of your finger.

6. Flour, egg and breadcrumb the goujons. Drop them individually into hot oil and fry in batches until crisp and golden.

Cutting steaks from large flatfish

See recipe on page 234.

1. Cut away the frills of the fish with scissors, then cut close around the back of the head, down to the backbone, so that you retain as much of the fillet as you can. Cut through the backbone behind the head using a cleaver and mallet, and then cut away the head.

2. Cut through the flesh along the backbone of the fish, down to the bone, with a sharp knife. Cut through the bone with the cleaver and mallet and then finish cutting the fish in half with the knife.

3. Cut each half into portion-sized tronçons, cutting through the backbone when necessary with the cleaver and mallet.

Cutting steaks from large round fish

1. Scale the fish and trim off the fins with scissors.

2. Wash out the cavity with plenty of cold water.

3. Cut the fish across, through the backbone, into steaks about 4cm thick, using a large, sharp knife.

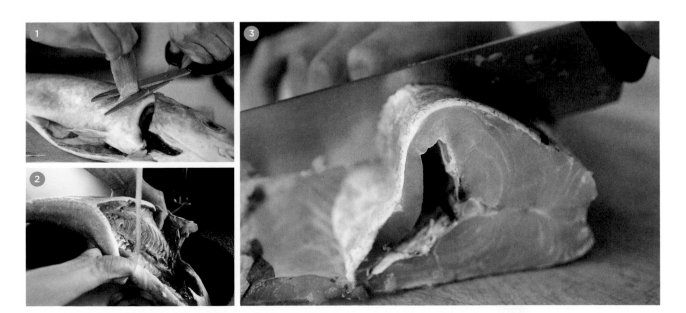

Skinning and pan-frying a whole flatfish

See recipe on page 238.

1. With kitchen scissors, cut away the frills from each side. Snip off all the other little fins.

2. Make a shallow cut through the skin across the tail end with a sharp knife. Push the tip of the knife under the skin to release a small flap.

3. Dip the fingers of one hand in salt and hold the tail. With your other hand, grab the flap of skin using a tea towel and, in one swift, sharp movement, pull the skin away. Repeat on the other side.

4. Season the skinned fish with salt and dip in flour, coating it well on both sides.

5. Pat the fish to remove the excess flour.

6. For each fish, heat 2 tablespoons of sunflower oil in a large frying pan. Add the fish, lower the heat slightly and add 7g unsalted butter pieces.

7. Fry for 4–5 minutes over a moderate heat until richly golden on the underside. Carefully turn the fish over and cook for a further 4–5 minutes.

8. Lift the fish on to a board. Working down first one side of the fish and then the other, trap the lateral bones with a thin-bladed, flexible knife and drag them away.

9. Now run the knife down the centre of the fish and gently ease the fillets away from the bones, but leave them attached along the outside edge.

10. Take hold of the bones at the head end and carefully 'unzip' the fish. The bones will come away cleanly and the fillets will fall back into place.

Preparing a whole ray

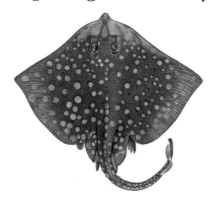

See recipe on page 240.

1. Make a cut 2.5cm behind the nose, right the way through the fish, then cut around both sides of the head and backbone, down to the tail. Separate the head from the backbone and tail and set it aside.

2. Separate the two wings where they are joined at the nose and deal with them one at a time.

3. Push the tip of the knife under the skin at what was the nose end to release a flap you can get hold of.

4. Grab hold of the flap of skin with fish pliers and start to tear it away from the surface of the wing.

5. When you have released enough skin, hold the wing down with a tea towel and sharply tear the rest completely away using the pliers. Repeat with the other side and the second wing.

6. Trim about 2.5cm away from the thinnest edge of each wing.

Removing ray cheeks

1. Lay the head dark-side down on a board and pull back the jaw to open up the mouth.

2. Slice diagonally under the jaw down towards the nose and remove the mouth piece.

3. The mouth piece will have the ray cheeks still attached.

4. Cut around the spherical cheek meats with the tip of a small sharp knife and remove.

5. These will still have a small piece of cartilage in the very centre that you can remove if you wish, but they are easier to get out once the cheeks have been cooked.

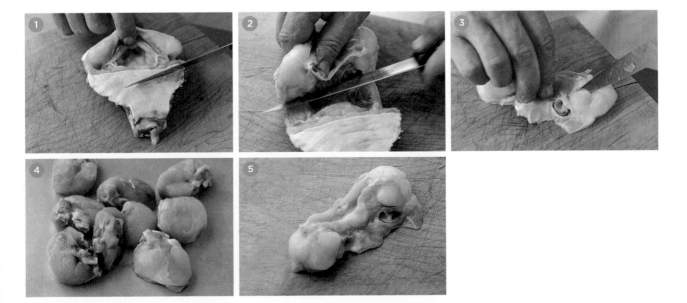

Skinning and filleting freshwater eel

1. Cut through the skin around the back of the head with a small sharp knife.

2. Using fish pliers, pull away about 2.5cm of skin from all the way around the head.

3. Hang the eel up by the head, with a meat hook or a piece of string, from something very secure and with plenty of room in which to work. Take a second pair of pliers, grab hold of some skin on each side of the eel and start to pull it away.

4. As soon as the skin starts to come away more cleanly, firmly and steadily pull it down towards the tail. As you near the tail it will start to get a little harder, but just give it a vigorous final tug and it will come away completely, over the tail.

5. To fillet the eel, lay it on a chopping board and cut off the head. Using a sharp, thin-bladed, flexible knife, make a shallow cut along the backbone of the fish, just above the line of bones. Start to cut away the fillet, keeping the blade of the knife as close to the bones as you can.

6. As soon as you can get the whole blade of the knife under the fillet, rest your other hand on top of the fish and cut the fillet away in one clean sweep, down towards the tail. Turn the eel over and repeat on the other side.

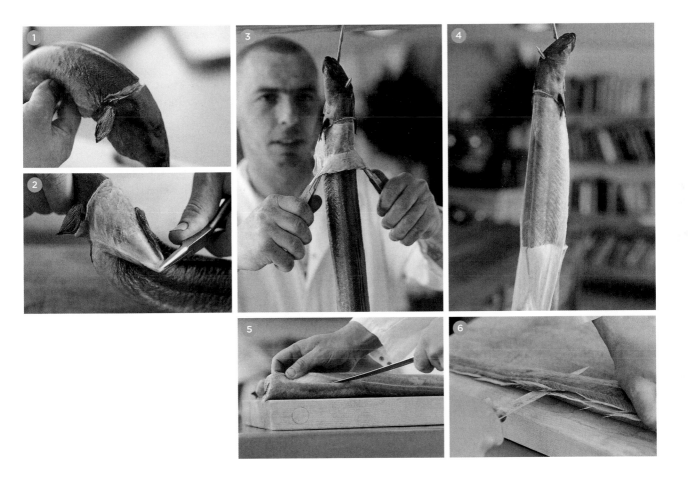

Making sushi

See recipe on page 123.

1. Flavour the cooked Japanese sticky rice with a sweet and salty vinegar mixture; add it gradually, lifting and folding the rice, so that it takes on a glossy sheen.

2. Wet your hands with lightly vinegared water and mould a 15g ball of rice mixture into a small rectangular block.

3. Slice a large skinned fillet of salmon into two along the natural muscle dividing line.

4. Slice into pieces 5mm thick.

5. Put a very small dot of wasabi paste on to your finger and spread it along the underside of each piece of fish.

6. Press the block of rice on to the fish.

7. Slit open the underside of each cooked prawn down to the tail and spread the cut face with a tiny amount of wasabi. Press together with a block of rice.

8. Wrap the remaining blocks of rice in a strip of nori. Secure the nori strip with a dab of water.

9. Spoon some keta, the large orange-red eggs of the salmon, on to the nori-wrapped rice.

Deep-frying small fry

See recipe on page 207.

1. Wash the small fry, then drain through a colander and shake well. Dry on kitchen paper. Tip into a bowl of flour seasoned with cayenne pepper and salt.

2. Toss in the flour until they are all well coated. Drop a large handful of fish into the frying basket and shake off the excess flour.

3. Lower the basket of fish into oil, heated to 190°C, and fry for 2–3 minutes until crisp and golden.

4. Remove the basket from the oil and drain the fish briefly on kitchen paper. Repeat. Tip them on to a warmed serving dish and serve with lemon wedges.

Sautéing fresh milt or roes

See recipe on page 213.

1. Dust the herring roes lightly in seasoned flour.

2. Melt some butter in a frying pan and, as soon as it begins to foam, add the roes.

3. Fry them over a medium-high heat for 2 minutes, turning once, until lightly golden. Serve at once.

Cutting escalopes from a salmon fillet

See recipe on page 202.

1. Fillet the salmon as described for large fish on page 22. Put the fillet skin-side down on a board with the narrowest end (the tail end) pointing towards you. Angle the blade of the knife down towards the skin and start to cut between the skin and the flesh, keeping the blade as close to the skin as you can. When the released fillet starts to get in the way, fold it back, take a firm hold of the skin and continue.

2. Remove the pin bones, which lie hidden in the flesh down the centre of the fillet: run your thumb along the line of bones in the opposite direction to which they are lying – they will then stand proud of the flesh. Pull them out with fish pliers or tweezers, or by trapping them between the point of a small, sharp knife and your thumb.

3. Put the fillet skinned-side down on to a board. Hold a long, thin-bladed knife at a 45-degree angle and cut the salmon into large 5mm-thick slices, called escalopes. To cook, brush the escalopes with oil, season and grill under a high heat for 30 seconds until only just firm.

Preparing a pavé of salmon

1. Put the fillet skinned-side down on a board. Remove the thinnest part of the belly flap and then neaten up the edges of the fillet with a sharp knife. Now cut the fillet across into neat rectangular pieces known as pavés (slabs), each weighing about 175g.

2. Lightly oil and season the pavés and put skinned-side down on to a smoking-hot ridged cast-iron griddle. Cook over a high heat, pressing them down gently now and then with a palette knife, until they have taken on rich golden bar marks underneath.

3. Sprinkle over some wine, leave them to cook for a few more seconds and then turn.

4. Cook on the other side for just 30 seconds or so, then remove the griddle from the heat and let them continue cooking in the residual heat of the pan for another 30 seconds. The salmon will remain quite rare inside.

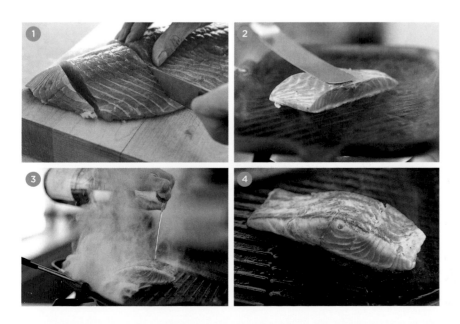

Poaching a whole fish in a fish kettle

1. Make a court-bouillon in a fish kettle (see page 310). Add the fish, bring back to a gentle simmer and leave it to poach for 16–18 minutes, or until the core temperature reaches 55°C using a thermometer. Then lift it out using the trivet, rest it on the sides of the kettle and allow the excess liquid to drain away.

2. Lift the fish on to a serving plate. Make a shallow cut through the skin along the backbone and around the back of the head.

3. Starting at the head end, peel back and remove the skin. Carefully turn the fish over and repeat on the other side.

4. Run a small knife down the length of the fish between the two fillets. Gently ease them apart and away from the bones.

5. Lift off the fillets in portion-sized pieces, then turn the fish over and repeat.

Baking a whole fish in foil

See recipe on page 194.

1. Put a prepared fish into the centre of a large sheet of foil which has been brushed with lots of melted butter.

2. Bring the edges of the foil up around the sides of the fish and scrunch it together at each end to form a canoe-shaped parcel. Carefully lift the parcel on to a large baking sheet.

3. Pour a mixture of melted butter, tarragon, white wine, lemon juice and seasoning into the cavity and over the top of the fish. Bring the sides of the foil parcel together over the top of the fish and seal really well to make a loose, airtight parcel. Bake in a hot oven at 220°C/gas 7 for 20–25 minutes, or until the core temperature reaches 55°C using a thermometer.

4. Remove the fish from the oven and open up the parcel. Carefully lift on to a plate and serve.

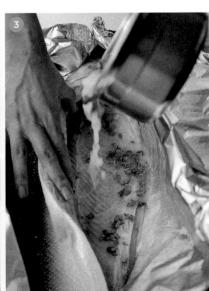

Confit of salmon

See recipe on page 190.

1. First remove the skin from the fillets.

2. Brush the fillets with olive oil.

3. Season with salt.

4. The best pan to use to confit the salmon is a fish kettle, using the trivet to weigh the bag down, but any large pan will do, using a smaller lid to keep the bag submerged. Heat the water to 50°C then remove from the heat.

5. Use a resealable bag. Put the fillets in the bag, press out as much air as possible and seal. Add to the pan and keep submerged for 20 minutes.

6. Remove from the water, open and check the core temperature with a thermometer. It should be 40–45°C. If not quite there, reseal the bag and return to the pan. If the temperature of the water in the pan slips below 50°C, reheat it.

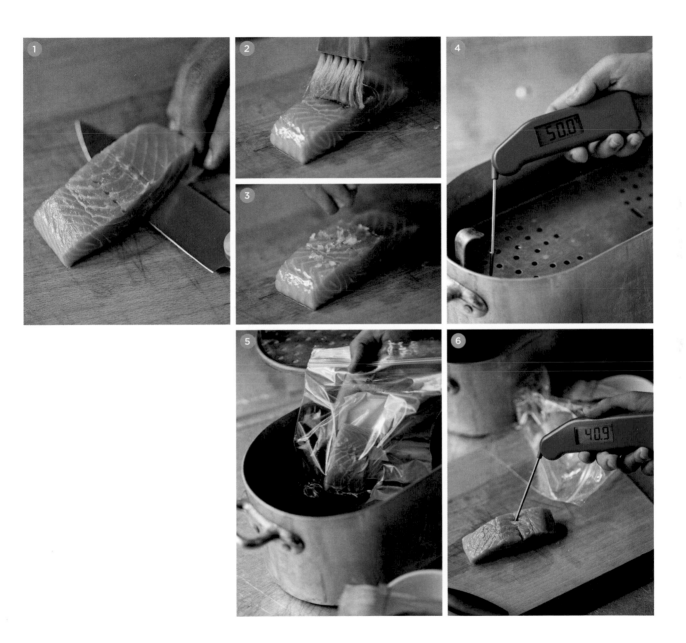

Crispy fish skin

1. Using a sharp knife, cut the skin away from the fillet.

2. Brush the pieces of skin on both sides with olive oil.

3. Sprinkle both sides with salt.

4. Put the fish on a baking sheet and top with another smaller one.

5. Weigh down with something heatproof like a cast-iron frying pan. Bake in a preheated hot oven at 200°C/gas 6 for 10 minutes.

6. Slice and use as a garnish for sashimi (see page 124) or the salmon with ponzu on page 199, or serve as a simple snack with beer. Keeps for a couple of days in a dry place.

Poaching smoked cod or haddock fillets in milk

1. Put some milk, or a mixture of milk and water, into a large shallow pan and add some bay leaves, onion and black peppercorns. Bring to the boil, add the smoked cod or smoked haddock fillets and bring back to a gentle simmer.

2. Poach the fish for 3–4 minutes until it is firm to the touch and the flesh has turned opaque, then remove. If serving in one piece, peel back and discard the skin. Otherwise, leave on a plate until cool enough to handle, then break into large flakes, discarding the skin and bones. Strain the poaching milk and use as the stock for a fish pie (see page 112), or freeze for later use.

Braising a whole large flatfish

1. Cut through the dark skin, all the way round the fish, close to the frill-like fins. This will make it easy to remove before serving and prevent it from splitting during cooking.

2. Season the fish lightly and place it in a large roasting tin with just enough water to prevent it from sticking – about 500ml. Braise, uncovered, in a hot oven for 30 minutes.

3. Transfer the fish to a warmed serving dish and carefully remove the head and the top skin. Reduce the remaining cooking juices to a few tablespoons and add to your sauce, then pour it right over the fish and take it to the table to serve.

4. Remove portion-sized pieces of the top fillets by sliding a palette knife under and lifting them off the bones. Then lift off the bones to give you access to the two bottom fillets.

Roasting a whole large round fish

See recipe on page 161.

1. Cut five or six shallow, diagonal slashes along the length of the prepared fish, first in one direction and then the other so that it becomes marked with a series of crosses.

2. Turn the fish over and repeat on the other side. This will help the heat to get through to the centre of the fish more quickly.

3. Place the fish on a base of pre-roasted vegetables in a large roasting tin. Bake until the fish is cooked through to the backbone: the temperature next to the bone should measure approximately 57–60°C.

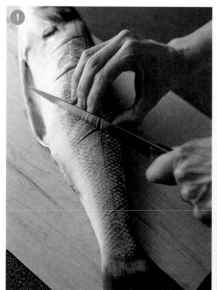

Baking fish in a pastry casing

See recipe on page 196.

1. Prepare two even-sized, thick pieces of skinned fish fillet (see page 22). Spread the inner face of one fillet with flavoured butter and lay the second fillet on top.

2. Roll out one sheet of puff pastry and place the fish in the centre. Brush a band of beaten egg around the fish.

3. Roll out a second piece of pastry into a rectangle roughly 5cm larger than the first one and lift it on top.

4. Press the pastry tightly around the outside of the salmon, taking care not to stretch it or trap in too much air; this might cause the pastry to shrink and the parcel to pop open when it's cooking. Press the edges together very firmly, then neatly trim them.

5. Mark all the way round with a fork – this ensures an even better seal. Decorate the top of the pastry with 'scales' using an upturned teaspoon and chill for 1 hour. Preheat the oven to 200°C/gas 6 and put in a baking sheet to heat up. Brush the pastry with beaten egg, and transfer to the hot baking sheet. Bake for 35–40 minutes, or until the core temperature reaches 55°C using a thermometer. Serve cut into slices.

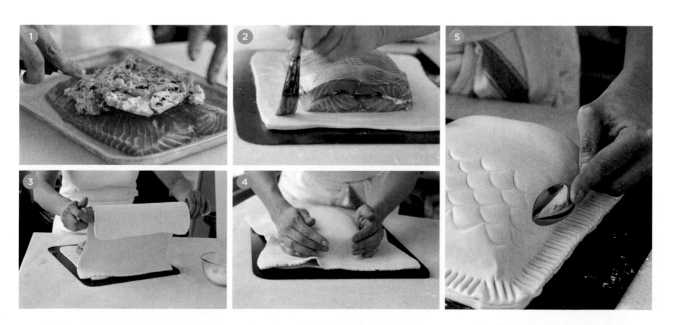

Baking fish in a salt crust

See recipe on page 162.

1. Mix about 1.5kg cooking salt with 2 egg whites. The mixture will look like wet sand.

2. Spread a thick layer of the salt mixture over the base of a shallow ovenproof dish or tin and put the fish on top. You don't need to remove the scales.

3. Completely cover the fish with the remaining salt mixture, making sure there are no gaps. Don't worry if the tails are still exposed. Bake the fish at 200°C/gas 6 for 20 minutes, or until the core temperature reaches 57–60°C using a thermometer.

4. Remove the fish from the oven and crack the top of the salt crust with the back of a large knife. Lift away the crust so that you can carefully lift out the fish.

5. Put the fish on to a serving plate. Make a shallow cut through the skin along the backbone and behind the head of the fish.

6. Pull the skin away from the top of the fish and lift off the two fillets. Turn the fish over and repeat on the other side.

Baking fillets 'en papillote'

See recipe on page 140.

1. Cut out four 40cm squares of greaseproof paper and foil. Put the foil squares on top of the paper ones and brush the centres with olive oil. Put 3 pieces of oven-roasted tomato slightly off-centre on each one, sprinkle with basil and top with the pieces of seasoned fish.

2. Bring the other side of the square over the fish so that all the edges meet. Starting at one end of the opening, fold over about 1cm of the edge, doing about 4cm at a time. Work your way all around the edge to make a semicircular parcel. Then go around again to make an even tighter seam.

3. Give the folded edge a good bash with a rolling pin. Put the parcels on to a baking sheet and bake at 240°C/gas 9 for 15 minutes.

4. As the fish cooks, the steaming juices will make the tightly sealed parcels puff up. Remove them from the oven, quickly transfer them to a warmed serving dish and take them to the table.

5. Slit open the parcels with the tip of a sharp knife.

6. Pull back the paper and foil from the baked fish.

7. Lift the fish and tomatoes on to warmed plates and pour over the cooking juices from the parcel. Spoon around a little tapenade and serve.

Making fish quenelles

See recipe on page 158.

1. Everything must be as cold as possible before you start. Put the fish fillets, butter, milk and breadcrumbs, nutmeg, lemon juice, egg and seasoning into a food processor.

2. Blend the mixture for at least 1 minute so that everything breaks down to form a very fine paste.

3. Transfer the mixture to a bowl and sit the bowl in a slightly larger one of well-iced water. Add the cream a little at a time, beating vigorously between each addition.

4. The finished mixture should be light and quite thick in texture. Cover and chill for 30 minutes.

5. Bring some lightly salted water to a gentle simmer in a wide shallow pan. Mould the mixture into 12 quenelles using two wet dessertspoons: take a heaped spoonful of mixture on to one spoon and scoop the mixture on to the other one by tucking the front edge of the empty spoon under the back edge of the mixture on the front one. Do this two or three times until you achieve a nice rugby-ball-shaped quenelle with a slight ridge running along the top. Drop them off the spoon into the water and poach gently for 3–4 minutes, turning them over halfway through.

6. Remove with a slotted spoon and drain briefly on a clean tea towel. Transfer them to individual gratin dishes and pour over the prepared sauce. Grill under a very high heat for 1 minute or until lightly browned.

Hot-smoking oily fish

See recipe on page 203.

1. Put the skinned fillets into a light brine (see page 203) and leave to cure for 20 minutes.

2. Put a thin layer of hardwood sawdust into the bottom of a wok and rest 6 wooden chopsticks over the top to act as a platform. Place the wok over a high heat until the sawdust begins to smoke. Then reduce the heat to low.

3. Rest a sushi mat (or something else that is permeable and will allow the smoke through) on the chopsticks and lay the fillets of fish on top. Cover the wok with a lid and smoke the fish for 3–4 minutes.

4. Uncover the wok and lift out the sushi mat and fish. With a palette knife, carefully lift the fish off the mat and on to a board. Cut into 4 even-sized pieces.

5. Brush the pieces of smoked fish with some olive oil.

6. Heat a ridged, cast-iron griddle until smoking-hot. Place the pieces of fish diagonally on to the griddle and cook for 30 seconds on each side or until lightly marked by the ridges. Serve warm.

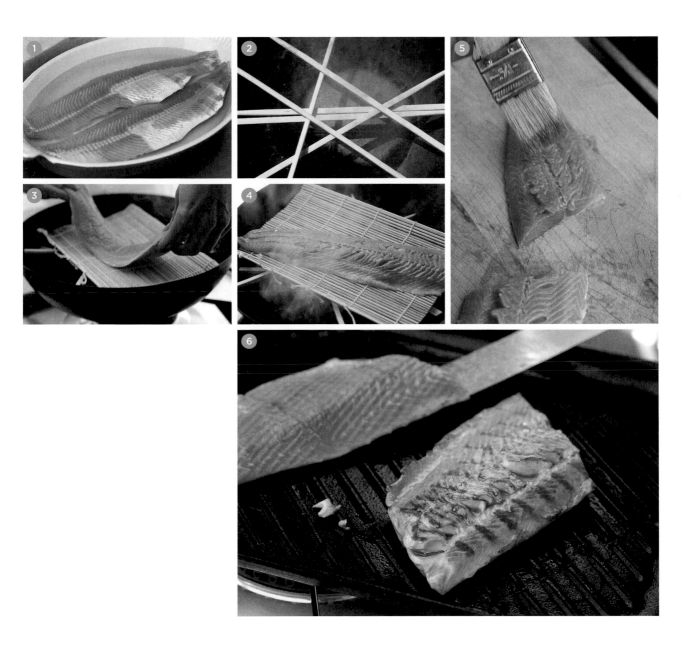

A Scandinavian cure for salmon

See recipe on page 193.

1. Put one unskinned salmon fillet skin-side down on to a large sheet of cling film. Thickly cover the cut face of the salmon with a mixture of chopped fresh dill, salt, sugar and crushed white peppercorns. You can cover this with another salmon fillet if you wish.

2. Tightly wrap the fish in 2 or 3 layers of cling film and lift it on to a large, shallow tray.

3. Place a chopping board on top of the fish and weigh it down. Refrigerate for 2 days, turning it every 12 hours so that the briny mixture bastes the outside of the fish. Replace the board and weights each time.

4. Unwrap the salmon and place it on a board. Slice on a 45-degree angle with a very sharp, long-bladed knife into very thin slices.

5. Carefully lift off the almost see-through slices as you cut them. These are now ready to serve.

Salting fresh cod

See recipe on page 134.

1. To salt your own cod, pour a 1cm-deep layer of salt over the base of a shallow plastic container. Put a thick piece of unskinned cod fillet on top and cover with another thick layer of salt. Cover and refrigerate overnight.

2. The next day, lift the now-rigid piece of cod out of the salt and rinse under cold water.

3. Put it into a large bowl and cover with lots of fresh water. Leave to soak for 1 hour. Commercially produced salt cod will be almost completely dried out and needs much longer soaking. Rinse off the excess salt and leave to soak in lots of cold water for 24–48 hours, depending on its thickness, changing the water now and then.

4. Drain the cod and remove the skin and bones. Simmer gently in water for 5 minutes, then lift out and drain well.

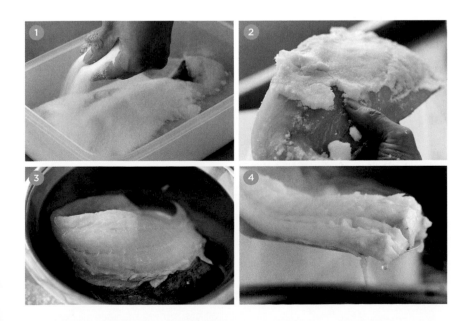

Preparing and butterflying raw prawns

1. Hold the body of the prawn in one hand and firmly twist off the head with the other. Save the heads for making stock (see page 310) if you wish.

2. Break open the soft shell along the underbelly of each prawn and peel it away from the flesh. You can leave the last tail segment of the shell in place for some recipes.

3. Run the tip of a small sharp knife along the back of the prawn and pull out the intestinal tract if dark and visible, but this is not always essential.

4. To butterfly raw prawns, make a deep cut down the back of each prawn with a small sharp knife, about halfway down into the meat. Brush the prawns with oil or melted butter, season and lay them on their sides on a lightly oiled baking tray. Grill for 2 minutes until cooked through.

Butterflying prawns in the shell

1. Remove the head if necessary (see opposite) and put the body belly-side up on a board. Cut each prawn in half through the shell to within 1cm of the tail.

2. Open up the prawns and lay them with the meat facing uppermost on a lightly oiled baking tray.

3. Brush them with oil or melted butter, season and grill under a high heat for about 2 minutes until cooked through.

Cooking a lobster and removing the meat

See recipe on page 303.

1. Put the lobster into the freezer 2 hours before cooking; this will kill it painlessly. Bring a large pan of heavily salted water to the boil (about 150g salt to every 5 litres water). Add the lobster and bring back to the boil. Cook a lobster up to 750g for 15 minutes and up to 1.25kg for 20 minutes. Remove and leave to cool.

2. Put the lobster belly-side down on to a board and make sure none of the legs is tucked underneath. Cut it in half, first through the middle of the head between the eyes. Then turn either the knife or the lobster around and finish cutting it in half through the tail.

3. Open it up and lift out the tail meat from each half.

4. Remove the intestinal tract from the tail meat.

5. Break off the claws and then break them into pieces at the joints. Crack the shells with a knife.

6. Remove the meat from each of the claw sections in as large pieces as possible.

7. Remove the soft greenish tomalley (liver) and any red roe from the head section of the shell with a teaspoon and save. Pull out the stomach sac and discard.

8. For lobster thermidor, cut the tail meat into smaller pieces and evenly distribute the tail and claw meat between the two shells with any roe. Transfer the cleaned half-shells on to a baking sheet.

9. Make a fish stock and cream reduction (see page 303). Stir the tomalley into the sauce. Spoon about 3 tablespoons of the sauce into each half-shell. Finish under a hot grill.

Removing lobster tail meat in one piece

1. Pull the tail away from the head.

2. Turn the tail section over and cut along either side of the flat belly-shell with strong scissors.

3. Lift back the flap of shell.

4. Lift out the tail meat. Remove the intestinal tract by running the knife down the back of the meat and removing it in one piece. Alternatively, you can cut the tail into thin slices and remove the intestinal tract from each slice with the tip of a small sharp knife.

Cooking langoustines or Dublin Bay prawns

See recipe on page 278.

1. Bring some salted water or prepared shellfish bouillon (see page 310) to the boil in a very large pan.

2. Add the langoustines to the pan and bring back to the boil.

3. Cook the langoustines for 2–5 minutes, depending on their size. Leave to cool.

4. Put each langoustine belly-side down on a board and cut it in half lengthways.

5. Scoop out the creamy contents of the head (the tomalley or liver) with a teaspoon. This can be mixed in with a dressing.

6. Arrange the halved langoustines cut-side up on a baking tray and brush with melted butter. Grill for 1–2 minutes until heated through.

Cutting up raw lobster for stir-frying

See recipe on page 304.

1. Kill the lobster painlessly as described on page 70. Cut it in half and remove the stomach sac and intestinal tract as described opposite, steps 1 to 3. Cut each tail half into 3 pieces.

2. Chop the claws from the head and cut each one into 2 pieces through the joint. Crack the shells with a large knife.

3. Snip off the antennae close to the head with scissors and discard.

4. Cut off the feeler-like legs as close to the shell as you can with scissors and discard also. Then cut each head section into 2 pieces.

5. Have all the pieces together on a tray ready to stir-fry as described on page 304.

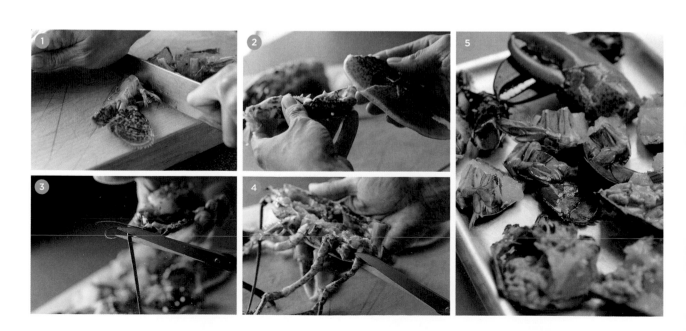

Halving a raw lobster for grilling

See recipe on page 301.

1. Kill the lobster painlessly as described on page 70. Lay the lobster belly-side down on a board and cut it in half.

2. Remove the stomach sac, a slightly clear pouch which will now be in half, from the head section of each half.

3. Remove the intestinal tract from the tail section (see page 72).

4. Put the lobster halves on to a baking tray and brush the meat with melted butter. Season with salt and pepper and grill under a medium-high heat for 8–10 minutes.

Killing and preparing a crab for steaming or stir-frying

See recipe on page 298.

1. Turn the crab on its back with its eyes facing you. Drive a thick skewer between the eyes into the centre of the crab. Lift up the tail flap and drive the skewer down though the centre of the body. When the crab is dead, its legs will go limp.

2. Break off the tail flap, and break off the claws close to the body.

3. Separate the body from the back shell by inserting a thick-bladed knife just above the mouth and twisting.

4. Pull the body away from the back shell.

5. Turn the body section over and pick off the feather-like gills (known as dead man's fingers).

6. Cut the body section in half.

7. Crack the claws using the back of the knife.

8. Use the blade of the knife to finish cutting through the joints.

9. Use the blade of the knife to crack the legs.

10. Spoon the brown meat out of the back shell on to a plate. Freeze and use later in a shellfish soup, seafood bisque or sauce. If making a stir-fry, such as Singapore chilli crab (see page 298), you can use up to a quarter in it. Too much makes the sauce grainy.

11. The pieces of crab are now ready for steaming or stir-frying. To steam, bring about 2.5cm of water to the boil in a wide shallow pan, pile the pieces of crab on to a petal steamer, lower into the pan and cover with a well-fitting lid. Steam for 10 minutes.

Cooking a crab and removing the meat

1. Kill the crab as described on page 76. Bring a large pan of heavily salted water to the boil (about 150g salt to every 5 litres water). Add the crab and bring back to the boil. Cook a crab weighing up to 550g for 15 minutes, up to 900g for 20 minutes, up to 1.5kg for 25 minutes, and any larger for 30 minutes. Remove and leave to cool.

2. Put the crab back-shell down on to a board and break off the claws.

3. Break off the legs, taking care to remove the knuckle joint too.

4. Lift up and break off the tail flap.

5. Push the blade of a large knife between the body and the back shell and twist the blade to release it.

6. Place your thumbs on either side of the body section and press firmly upwards until it comes away.

7. Pull the feather-like gills, known as the dead man's fingers, off the body and discard.

8. Scoop out the brown meat from the centre of the body section with a teaspoon and keep it separate from the white meat.

9. Cut the body section in half using a large knife.

Continued overleaf

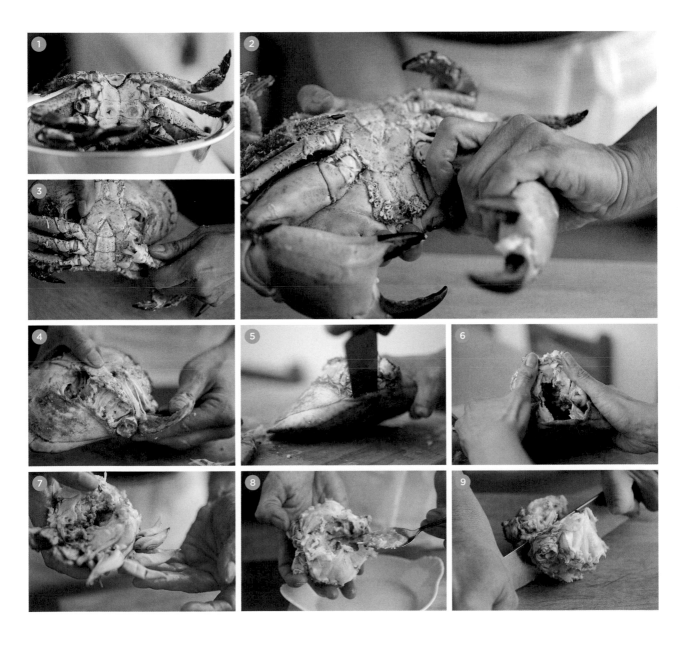

10. Remove the white meat from all the little channels with a crab pick.

11. When all the meat has been removed, you should be left with a hollow and much lighter piece of shell.

12. Crack the shell of the claws with the back of a knife and remove the meat. Remove the thin piece of bone concealed within the meat of the pincers. Break the shell of the legs with crackers and hook out the white meat with the crab pick.

13. Put the back shell on to a board with the eyes and mouth facing you. Press on the little piece of shell located just behind the eyes until it snaps. Lift out and discard the mouth piece and stomach sac.

14. Scoop out the brown meat from the back shell (which is sometimes quite wet and sometimes more solid) with a spoon. Add it to that from the body, unless you are using white meat only, for example to make crab cakes.

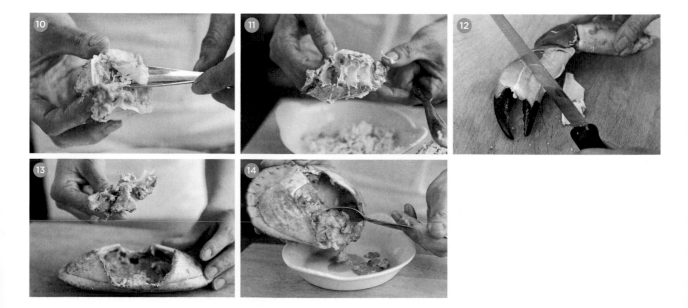

Making crab cakes

See recipe on page 296.

1. Add some finely crushed cracker crumbs to the white crab meat to absorb any excess moisture in the meat.

2. Make a binding mixture of beaten egg, mayonnaise, mustard, lemon juice, Worcestershire sauce and some seasoning.

3. Fold this through the crab meat, taking care not to break up the lumps of crab too much, then stir in some parsley.

4. Shape the mixture into eight patties about 8cm across. Put them on to a plate, cover and chill for at least 1 hour to help them firm up.

5. Pour some clarified butter into a well-seasoned or non-stick frying pan and leave it to get hot.

6. Add the crab cakes to the pan and fry them over a medium heat for 2–3 minutes on each side until crisp and golden.

Making a clear crab soup

See recipe on page 106.

1. Flavour a pan of chicken stock with fresh ginger, lime zest, lime juice, lemongrass, chilli, fish sauce and soy sauce. Add the pieces of prepared crab (see page 76) and prawn shells.

2. Bring the stock to the boil, cover and leave to simmer gently for 25 minutes, to extract the flavour from the crab.

3. Strain the stock into a clean pan and leave it to cool. Meanwhile, remove the meat from the crab claws and set aside.

4. Add some very finely chopped inexpensive white fish fillet, such as coley, some thinly sliced leek and 2 egg whites to the cooled stock. The egg whites clarify the stock by trapping fine particles into a crust that can be removed.

5. Return the pan to a medium heat and whisk steadily until the mixture comes back to the boil. Then stop whisking immediately and leave to simmer very gently for 5 minutes, during which time the crust will form on top.

6. Slowly pour the stock through a muslin-lined sieve into a clean pan. Finally, let the crust slide into the sieve and leave until all the liquid has dripped through. Briefly cook the prawns, some thinly sliced monkfish and some prepared vegetables in the clarified stock. Finish with some noodles and the reserved crab meat.

Using crab shells and meat for making a bisque

See recipe on page 107.

1. Wash the crabs well under cold running water. Prepare them and cook in a pan of well-salted boiling water (see page 76) for 2 minutes, then drain.

2. Chop up the crabs very roughly with a large knife into smallish pieces.

3. Add the crab pieces and a splash of cognac to a pan of lightly sautéed vegetables.

4. Fry the crab pieces for 3–4 minutes, stirring now and then, until all the liquid has evaporated. Add some tomatoes, tomato purée, white wine, tarragon and fish stock to the pan. Bring to the boil, lower the heat and leave to simmer, uncovered, for 30 minutes.

5. Briefly liquidize the soup in batches until the shells have broken down into pieces about the size of a fingernail. It should not be completely smooth. Then strain through a conical sieve into a clean pan.

6. Press as much liquid as you can from the debris with the back of a ladle and then discard everything that is left in the sieve.

7. Strain the soup once more through a fine sieve to remove the finer debris. Bring it back to the boil, and reduce a little to concentrate the flavour if necessary. Add some cream and season to taste with lemon juice, cayenne pepper and salt.

Cleaning and steaming mussels

See recipe on page 256.

1. Wash the mussels under plenty of cold running water. Discard any that are open and won't close up when lightly squeezed. Pull out the tough fibrous beards or 'byssus' protruding from between the tightly closed shells.

2. Knock off any barnacles with a large knife and give the mussels another quick rinse to remove any little bits of shell.

3. Put the mussels into a very large pan with liquid as given in the recipe. Never more than half-fill the pan. If the pan is overcrowded, those at the bottom will overcook before the heat can reach those at the top.

4. Cover and cook the mussels over a high heat, shaking the pan vigorously every now and then, for 3–4 minutes until they have all just opened.

5. Immediately remove the pan from the heat and spoon the mussels into deep bowls.

Opening mussels for serving raw

1. Push the tip of a small knife between the shells on the straighter side. Run the tip all around the edge.

2. Ease back the top shell and run the tip of the knife around its inside edge to release the meat, taking care not to tear the flesh.

3. Pull back the top shell and snap it off if you wish.

Removing the meat from large clams

1. Wash the clams under plenty of cold running water. Put them in a single layer into the bottom of a large shallow pan and add a little water.

2. Cover the pan with a well-fitting lid and cook over a high heat for 2–3 minutes or until the clams have opened just enough for you to get them out of the shells. You don't want to cook them completely.

3. Remove the clams from the pan, reserving the liquor if it's required, and leave them to cool slightly. Then slide a small sharp knife into each shell and cut through the two muscles on either side near the hinge, which hold the two shells together.

4. Remove the meats from the bottom shells and chop them into small pieces.

Preparing small clams for serving raw

1. Slide the sharp edge of a small knife between the two tightly closed shells, on the opposite side to the hinge.

2. Draw the blade of the knife back so that only the tip is inside the clam. Run just the very tip of the knife right the way round the edge of the shell so as not to damage the meat inside. You will eventually feel the resistance give way.

3. Run the blade around the top inside edge of the clam to release the meat from the top shell. Carefully pull back the top shell so as not to damage the meat, releasing it where necessary if still attached. Release the meat from the bottom shell and snip off the shell if you wish.

4. Arrange the clams on a plate of crushed ice and seaweed, and serve.

Preparing scallops

See recipe on page 268.

1. Wash the scallops to remove any sand and weed from the shells. Hold a scallop in one hand, with the flat shell facing uppermost, and slide the blade of a sharp, thin-bladed, flexible knife between the two shells. You may want to wrap the hand holding the scallop in a tea towel for safety.

2. Keeping the blade of the knife flat against the top shell, feel for the ligament that joins the meat of the scallop to the shell. Cut through it and lift off the top shell.

3. Pull out the frilly 'skirt' and black stomach sac which surrounds the white scallop meat and pink coral. Rinse away any sand from inside the shell.

4. Slide the knife under the scallop meat, keeping the blade close to the shell, and cut it away. Pull off and discard the small white ligament attached to the side of the scallop meat.

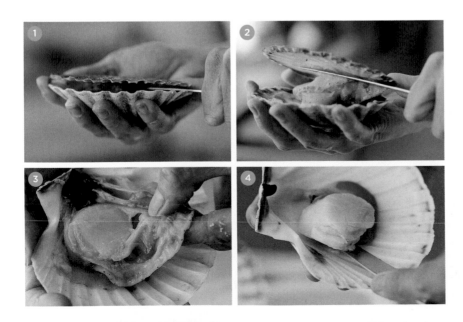

Opening oysters

See recipe on page 264.

1. Wrap one hand in a tea towel and hold the oyster in it, flat shell facing uppermost. Push the point of an oyster knife into the hinge, located at the narrowest point.

2. Work the knife back and forth quite forcefully until the hinge breaks and you can slide the knife in between the two shells.

3. Twist the point of the knife upwards to lever up the top shell and locate the ligament that joins the oyster meat to it. It will be slightly right of the centre of the top shell. Cut through it with the knife and lift off the top shell. Keep the bottom shell upright so as not to lose the juices. Release the oyster meat from the bottom shell and pick out any little pieces of shell.

Preparing squid for stir-frying

See recipe on page 114.

1. Hold the squid's body in one hand and the head with the other and gently pull the head away from the body, taking the milky white intestines with it.

2. Remove the tentacles from the head by cutting them off just in front of the eyes. Discard the head and separate the tentacles if they are large.

3. Squeeze out the beak-like mouth from the centre of the tentacles and discard it.

4. If you want to retain the ink sac, look amongst the intestines for a very small, pearly-white pouch with a slight blue tinge and carefully cut it away.

5. Reach into the body and pull out the clear, plastic-like quill.

6. Pull off the two fins from either side of the body pouch. Then pull away the brown, semitransparent skin from both the body and the fins. Wash out the body pouch with water.

7. Insert the blade of a sharp, thin-bladed, flexible knife into the opening of the body pouch and slit it open along one side. Open it out flat and pull away any left-over intestines and membrane.

8. Score what was the inner side with the tip of a small sharp knife into a diamond pattern, taking care not to cut too deeply. Then cut it into 5cm pieces.

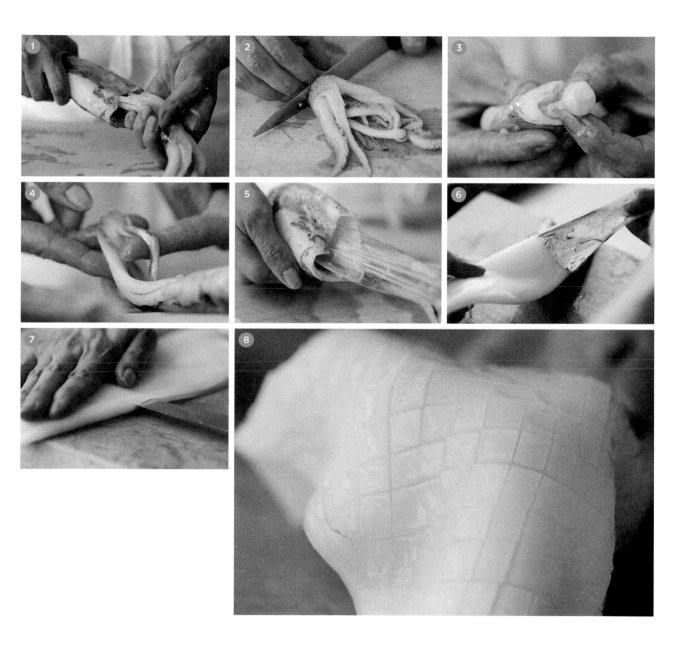

Tenderizing tough octopus in the oven

See recipe on page 244.

1. In Britain, you can buy the common octopus (*Octopus vulgaris*), which only needs simmering for 45 minutes. For other types, this is a simple way to tenderize it. First, turn the body of the octopus inside out.

2. Pull away and discard the entrails. Remove the bonelike strips sticking to the sides of the body.

3. Locate the stomach sac, which is about the size of an avocado stone, and cut it away.

4. Wash the octopus well inside and out and then turn the body right side out again. Press out the beak and soft surround from the centre of the tentacles and cut it out with the tip of a small knife.

5. Put the prepared octopus into a shallow casserole dish ready for tenderizing in the oven.

6. Pour over some olive oil, cover with a well-fitting lid and cook in a cool oven set at 150°C/gas 2 for 2 hours until very tender.

Cleaning cuttlefish

See recipe on page 246.

1. Cut off the tentacles, just in front of the eyes. Remove the beak-like mouth from the centre of the tentacles and discard.

2. Separate the tentacles and pull the skin from each one.

3. Pull the tough skin away from the body section.

4. Run a sharp knife down the centre of the back and lift out the cuttlebone.

5. Open up the body pouch. Locate the pearly-white ink sac in amongst the entrails and remove it carefully. This is worth freezing and using later to flavour and colour a black risotto or pasta. Remove and discard the rest of the entrails and head. Wash the body well and then cut it in half lengthways.

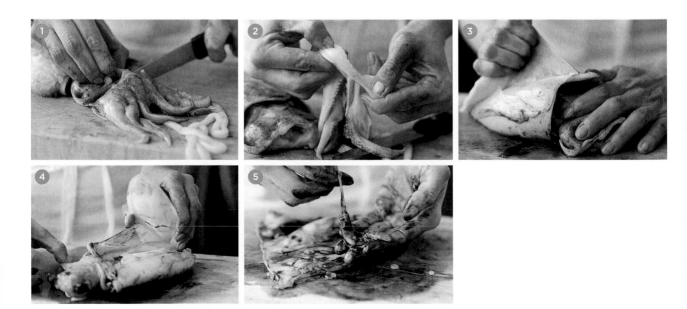

Preparing sea urchins

See recipe on page 273.

1. Wrap one hand in a tea towel and hold the sea urchin in it with the mouth (the soft part in the centre) facing uppermost. Push one blade of a pair of scissors into the mouth and cut around it to release a 5–8cm disc of shell. Alternatively, cut off a 2.5cm slice of the sea urchin with a large serrated knife.

2. Lift away the disc of shell and pour away any liquid from inside the urchin.

3. Pull out all the black parts from inside the shell, leaving behind the small clusters of orange roe.

4. Scoop out the individual clusters of roe with a teaspoon, keeping them as whole as possible. Add them to hot cooked pasta and turn over gently once or twice. The residual heat will be sufficient to lightly cook the roe. Alternatively, fold the roes into scrambled egg and serve in the washed-out shells.

RECIPES

CHAPTER ONE

Mixed seafood

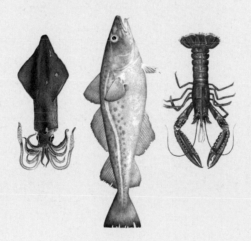

Classic fish soup with rouille and croûtons

Alternative fish:
any except for oily fish
like herring, kingfish,
mackerel or salmon

SERVES 4
1kg mixed fish such as
   gurnard, conger eel,
   cod and grey mullet
1.2 litres water
90ml olive oil
75g each onion, celery,
   leek and fennel, roughly
   chopped
3 garlic cloves, sliced
Juice of ½ orange plus
   2 strips of orange zest
200g canned chopped
   tomatoes
1 red pepper,
   seeded and sliced
1 bay leaf
1 sprig of thyme
A pinch of saffron strands
½ tsp chilli flakes
100g unpeeled prawns
Salt and freshly ground
   black pepper

For the croûtons
1 small baguette
Olive oil, for frying
1 garlic clove
½ quantity Rouille
   (see page 311)
25g Parmesan cheese,
   finely grated

I love fish soup. It's a deeply satisfying dish. You can use almost any fish for this apart from the oily ones.

Fillet all the fish as described on pages 20–28. Use the bones with the water to make a fish stock (see page 310).

Heat the olive oil in a large pan, add the vegetables and garlic and cook gently for 20 minutes until soft but not coloured. Add the orange zest, tomatoes, red pepper, bay leaf, thyme, saffron, chilli flakes and prawns, and the fish fillets. Cook briskly for 2–3 minutes, then add the strained stock and orange juice, bring to the boil and simmer for 40 minutes.

Meanwhile, for the croûtons, thinly slice the baguette on the diagonal and fry the slices in the olive oil until crisp and golden. Drain on kitchen paper and rub one side of each piece with the garlic clove.

Liquidize the soup, then pass it through a sieve into a clean pan, pressing out as much liquid as possible with the back of a ladle. Return the soup to the heat and season to taste.

To serve, ladle the soup into warmed bowls and leave each person to spread rouille on to the croûtons, float them on their soup and sprinkle them with Parmesan cheese.

I can never resist slipping a chowder into my seafood books – I love the subtle combination of seafood, salt pork and cream.

Cod and lobster chowder

Alternative seafood: any flaky white fish and prawns or scallops

SERVES 4

450–550g lobster, freshly cooked
4 water biscuits
50g butter, softened
100g salt pork or rindless streaky bacon, finely diced
1 small onion, finely chopped
15g plain flour
1.2 litres milk
2 potatoes (about 200g), peeled and diced
1 bay leaf
450g thick cod fillet, skinned
120ml double cream
A pinch of cayenne pepper
Sea salt and freshly ground black pepper
2 tbsp chopped parsley, to serve

Remove the meat from the cooked lobster: see page 70.

Crush 2 of the water biscuits to very fine crumbs with a rolling pin. Then mix with the tomalley (liver), other soft material from the lobster head and half the butter; or blend everything to a paste in a small food processor.

Heat the rest of the butter in a medium-sized pan, add the pork or bacon and fry over a medium heat until lightly golden. Add the onion and cook gently until softened. Stir in the flour and cook for 1 minute. Gradually stir in the milk, then the potatoes and bay leaf, and simmer for 10 minutes. Add the cod and simmer for 4–5 minutes. Then lift the fish out of the milk, break the flesh into large flakes with a wooden spoon and return to the soup. Stir in the water-biscuit paste, lobster meat and cream and simmer for 1 minute. Season with the cayenne pepper, 1 teaspoon of salt and some black pepper.

To serve, coarsely crush the 2 remaining biscuits and sprinkle them over the soup with the chopped parsley.

Seafood in a crab and ginger broth

See technique on page 82.

Alternative seafood: blue swimming, spider or mud crab, langoustines, lobster, Moreton Bay or Balman bugs

SERVES 4

2.5cm fresh ginger
2 limes
1.7 litres Chicken stock
  (see page 310)
1 fat lemongrass stalk
1 red bird's-eye chilli
1 tbsp fish sauce
1 tbsp light soy sauce
1 small cooked brown crab,
  about 500g–750g
8 headless raw prawns
25g rice vermicelli noodles
100g monkfish fillet,
  thinly sliced
2 spring onions, cut into 5cm
  pieces and finely shredded
25g bok choi, in 2.5cm pieces
25g beansprouts

To clarify the stock
100g coley or other
  inexpensive white fish,
  skinned and finely chopped
1 small leek, thinly sliced
2 egg whites

To serve
Chopped mint and coriander
  leaves, plus extra to garnish
2 bird's-eye chillies, sliced
2 tbsp rice wine vinegar or
  white wine vinegar

I devised this recipe to make use of all the flavour in crab and prawn shells that are normally just thrown away. That, and the fact that I love a delicate, clear soup as a first course.

Cut the ginger into very thin slices. Remove a strip of zest from one of the limes, then squeeze the juice from both.

Pour the chicken stock into a large pan and add three-quarters of the sliced ginger, the lime zest and juice, the outer leaves of the lemongrass, the bird's-eye chilli sliced lengthways, and the fish sauce and soy sauce. Bring to the boil.

Meanwhile, prepare the crab as described on page 78. Peel and devein the prawns, reserving the shells (see page 68).

Add the crab legs, body and back shell, but not the claws, to the boiling stock with the prawn shells. Bring back to the boil, cover and simmer very gently for 25 minutes, adding the claws after 20 minutes.

Pour the stock through a large sieve into another large pan, discarding all the solids except for the crab. Leave the stock to cool, then clarify it using the coley, leek and egg whites, as shown on page 82.

Remove the white meat from the claws, legs and main body of the crab in pieces as large as possible. Soak the noodles in boiling salted water for 2 minutes, then drain. Finely chop the remaining ginger slices and the lemongrass core.

Bring the clarified stock up to a gentle simmer and add the prawns, monkfish, ginger and lemongrass. Cook for 1 minute. Add the noodles, crab meat, spring onions, bok choi and beansprouts and simmer for 30 seconds, then remove from the heat.

Mix the mint and coriander together in one small bowl and the chillies and vinegar in another.

Divide the noodles between 4 large soup plates. Ladle the soup over them, garnish with coriander leaves and serve with bowls of chopped herbs and chilli vinegar.

The little crabs you can find on the beach are almost as good as lobsters for making bisque. Bisques are soups made with both the shells and meat of shellfish.

Shore crab bisque

See technique on page 84.

Alternative seafood:
any crab or prawns

SERVES 4
1kg shore crabs, washed
50g butter
50g each onion, carrot and
   celery, finely chopped
1 bay leaf
2 tbsp cognac
4 tomatoes
1 tsp tomato purée
75ml dry white wine
1 sprig of tarragon
1.75 litres Fish stock
   (see page 310)
4 tbsp double cream
A pinch of cayenne pepper
2 tsp lemon juice
Salt and freshly ground
   black pepper

Bring a large pan of well-salted water to the boil. Add the crabs, bring back to the boil and cook for 2 minutes. Drain, leave to cool slightly, then chop up roughly with a large knife.

Melt the butter in a large heavy-based pan and add the chopped vegetables and the bay leaf. Cook for 3–4 minutes without letting them brown.

Add the crabs and the cognac and cook until all the liquid has evaporated.

Add the tomatoes, tomato purée, wine, tarragon and stock. Bring to the boil and simmer for 30 minutes.

Briefly liquidize the soup in batches until the shells have broken down into pieces about the size of your fingernail. Strain through a conical strainer into a clean pan, pressing out as much liquid as you can with the back of a ladle. Then pass it once more through a very fine sieve.

Bring the soup back to the boil, and reduce a little to concentrate the flavour if desired. Then lower the heat, add the cream, cayenne pepper and lemon juice and season to taste.

Bourride of red mullet, gurnard and fresh salted cod

Alternative fish:
barramundi, bass, blue
cod, blue-eye trevalla, bream,
dhufish, flathead, flounder,
grey mullet, John Dory,
kinglip, mahi mahi,
snapper, whiting

SERVES 4
200–250g skin-on red
    mullet fillet
200–250g skin-on gurnard
200–250g Fresh salted cod
    (see page 67)
2 tbsp olive oil
1 medium onion, chopped
1 small leek, cleaned and
    chopped
½ fennel bulb, chopped
4 garlic cloves, chopped
2 thick strips of orange zest
2 tomatoes, sliced
1 bay leaf and 1 sprig of thyme
1.2 litres Fish stock
    (see page 310)
½ tsp salt
1 quantity Aïoli (see page 311)

For the croûtons
2 tbsp olive oil
4 x 2.5cm-thick slices
    baguette, cut on the slant
Harissa (see page 311)

Bourride was my first experience of a Provençale fish stew in the late 1970s, and is much easier to do well than bouillabaisse.

First, make the croûtons. Heat the oil in a frying pan and fry the bread on both sides until crisp and golden. Spread the croûtons with harissa, and keep warm.

For the bourride, cut all the fish into 50g pieces. Heat the oil in a large pan. Add the onion, leek, fennel, garlic and orange zest and fry gently without colouring for 5 minutes. Add the tomatoes, bay leaf, thyme, fish stock and salt, bring to the boil and simmer for 30 minutes.

Add the fish pieces and simmer gently for 5 minutes, then carefully lift them out on to a warmed serving dish and keep warm.

Strain the cooking liquor through a fine sieve into a clean pan, pressing out as much liquid as you can with the back of a ladle. Put the aïoli into a bowl and whisk in a ladle of the cooking liquor. Stir the mixture back into the pan and cook over a low heat until slightly thickened. Do not let it boil.

Pour the sauce over the fish. Serve with the croûtons.

Le plateau de fruits de mer

SERVES 2
1 x 500g cooked lobster
1 x 500g cooked brown crab
2 native oysters
2 Pacific oysters
12 mussels, cleaned
    (see page 86)
12 carpetshell clams,
    washed
12 winkles
2 whelks
6 cooked Dublin Bay prawns
    (langoustines) (see page 73)
4 cooked Mediterranean
    prawns (crevettes)

To serve
50ml red wine
50ml red wine vinegar
1 shallot, finely chopped
½ quantity Mayonnaise
    (see page 311), made
    with olive oil
Plenty of crushed ice
500g samphire or
    bladderwrack seaweed,
    washed (optional)
1 lemon, cut in half

A centrepiece dish for a long leisurely lunch in convivial company. A wonderful aspect of this dish is that it also gives importance to all those little, unloved shellfish and crustaceans like winkles and whelks. The seafood in the ingredients is just a suggestion. It's what we use at the Seafood Restaurant, but just oysters and prawns with mayonnaise is lovely. The advantage of samphire as an optional decoration is that you can eat it.

Cut the lobster lengthways in half (see page 70). Cut the crab in half right through the back shell, down between the eyes. Open the oysters as described on page 91 and the raw mussels and clams as shown on pages 87 and 89, or steam them open briefly in a hot saucepan with a splash of water, with the lid on. If the winkles and whelks are raw, drop them into separate pans of boiling salted water and cook the winkles for 1 minute and the whelks for 4 minutes, then drain.

Mix together the red wine, vinegar and shallot and pour into a small bowl. Spoon the mayonnaise into another bowl.

To assemble the dish, cover the base of a large serving platter with a thick layer of crushed ice and cover with the samphire or seaweed. Arrange the shellfish and prawns on top and garnish with the halved lemon. Serve with the shallot vinegar and mayonnaise.

A seafood velouté with a crisp breadcrumb topping
flavoured with a hint of truffle oil. I fry the fish first so
that it doesn't thin the creamy sauce in the pie as it cooks.

Newlyn fish pie

Suitable fish:
blue cod, blue-eye
trevalla, cod, monkfish,
hake, pollack, snapper

Suitable seafood:
crab, lobster, peeled
prawns, scallops

SERVES 4-6
200g finely chopped onion
60g butter
1 quantity Velouté
    (see page 311), made with
    2 bay leaves, 1 crushed
    clove, 1 pinch freshly
    grated nutmeg
30g Parmesan cheese, grated
50ml double cream
Juice of ½ lemon
Salt
500g mixed seafood: aim for
    ¾ fish fillet and ¼ shellfish
    or crustaceans, such as
    prawns, lobster or crab
50g flour
30ml vegetable oil
10g butter
100g button mushrooms,
    thinly sliced
1 tsp French mustard
1 tsp truffle oil

For the crust
50g Japanese panko
    breadcrumbs or fresh
    breadcrumbs dried out for
    10 minutes in a hot oven
30g melted butter

Preheat the oven to 180°C/gas 4. Slow-cook the onion in the
butter in a saucepan for 10 minutes.

Make the velouté as on page 311 but adding the bay leaves,
clove and nutmeg. Pour the velouté through a sieve into the
sautéed onions and add the Parmesan cheese, double cream
and lemon juice, and a little salt if necessary.

Cut the fish fillet into bite-size pieces, 3–4cm long. Season
with a little salt and turn over in the flour. Fry for 2–3 minutes in
a frying pan over a medium heat using the vegetable oil and butter.
Remove the fish to your pie dish. Fry the mushrooms in the same
pan adding a little salt; stir in the mustard and add to the pie dish.
Now add the shellfish or crustaceans to the pie dish. They can be
raw or cooked, but if raw scallops or prawns are large, slice them
in half. Drizzle the truffle oil over.

Pour the sauce over the fish. Mix the breadcrumbs with the
melted butter, and spread over the top. Bake for 20 minutes.

Salad of stir-fried prawns, pork and squid with glass noodles, chilli and mint

SERVES 4
Vegetable oil, for frying
100g shallots, thinly sliced
200g dried glass noodles
200g large raw prawns,
    peeled (see page 68)
200g prepared medium
    squid (see page 92),
    sliced across into
    5mm-thick rings and
    the tentacles separated
    into pairs
100g minced pork
50g roasted peanuts,
    coarsely chopped
20g mint leaves,
    finely shredded
25g dried shrimp
1 red bird's-eye chilli,
    finely chopped
4 tbsp lime juice
1 tbsp palm sugar
3 tbsp fish sauce

South-east Asian salads like this are a great balance of salty, sweet-sour and spicy. It's important to have both pork and seafood, but you can vary the seafood from prawns and squid to crab meat or even small pieces of firm fish such as monkfish, John Dory or gurnard.

Pour 1cm oil into a large deep frying pan. Add the shallots and fry over a medium heat until crisp and golden brown. Lift out with a slotted spoon on to plenty of kitchen paper and leave to drain. Reserve the frying oil.

Bring a large pan of unsalted water to the boil, add the noodles, take the pan off the heat and leave to soak for 2 minutes. Drain well, roughly cut up the noodles and set aside to drain even further.

Heat 2 tablespoons of the shallot-flavoured oil in a wok or pan, add the prawns, season lightly with salt and stir-fry for 2 minutes or until just cooked. Lift on to a plate. Add another 1–2 tablespoons oil to the pan, then add the squid, season lightly with salt and stir-fry for 1–1½ minutes until caramelized. Transfer to the plate with the prawns. Finally, heat another 1–2 tablespoons oil in the pan, add the minced pork and stir-fry for 1½–2 minutes, breaking it up with a wooden spoon into small pieces as it browns.

Put the noodles into a large bowl and add the pork, prawns, squid, peanuts, mint, dried shrimp and chilli and toss together well. Mix the lime juice, sugar and fish sauce together, toss through the salad and serve at room temperature.

You can use Arborio, Carnaroli, Maratelli or Vialone rice for a good risotto. For added flavour use fish or chicken stock instead of water to make the risotto stock.

Seafood risotto

Alternative seafood: cuttlefish, hapuka, John Dory, snapper

SERVES 4
500g prawns
36 smallish mussels
100g monkfish fillet
    (see page 25), thinly sliced
50g cleaned squid
    (see page 92), thinly sliced

For the stock
25ml olive oil
1 garlic clove, chopped
1 medium carrot, chopped
1 celery stick, chopped
1 small onion, chopped
1 small leek, chopped
¼ red chilli, chopped
1 tomato, chopped
A small pinch of
    saffron threads
1.5 litres water or
    Fish or Chicken stock
    (see page 310)
Cooking liquor from
    the mussels

For the risotto
50g unsalted butter
2 shallots, chopped
1 garlic clove, chopped
350g risotto rice
125ml dry white wine
Extra virgin olive oil

Peel and devein the prawns as shown on page 68, reserving the shells for the stock. Prepare and steam the mussels in a splash of water in a pan, following the instructions on page 86. Keep the cooking liquor for the stock. Remove the meats from all but 8 of the shells – a few whole mussels in the risotto look very appetizing.

To make the stock, heat the oil in a large pan and add the garlic, carrot, celery, onion, leek and chilli. Fry for 5 minutes without colouring. Add the reserved prawn shells and cook for another couple of minutes, then add the tomato, saffron, water or stock and mussel liquor. Bring to the boil and simmer for 30 minutes with the lid off, then push through a conical sieve with the back of a ladle to extract plenty of flavour. You should end up with about 1 litre.

To make the risotto, melt the butter in a heavy-based pan, then add the shallots and garlic and sweat until softened. Add the rice and stir for a couple of minutes until well coated with butter. Pour in the wine. Bring to the boil and simmer until all the wine has disappeared.

Add the stock to the rice in three stages, allowing the liquid to be absorbed each time before adding the next. Stir continuously until the stock is almost completely absorbed, by which time the rice will be just tender but still firm to the bite.

While the risotto is cooking, brush the rest of the seafood with olive oil and grill for 3–4 minutes. To serve, carefully mix a tablespoon or two of extra virgin olive oil and the seafood, including the mussels, into the risotto leaving a few pieces on top.

Indonesian seafood curry

*Alternative fish:
flathead, grouper,
grunter, luderick,
morwong*

SERVES 4

400g fish fillets, such as
   monkfish, John Dory,
   barramundi, gurnard
   or sea bass
250g medium squid
   (pouches about 18cm long)
12 large raw prawns
1 tsp salt
Freshly ground white pepper
1 tbsp lime juice
200g (8 heaped tbsp)
   Indonesian spice paste
   (basa gede, see page 314)
2 tbsp vegetable oil
4 kaffir lime leaves,
   torn into small pieces
2 fat lemongrass stalks,
   halved and bruised
120ml Asian chicken stock
   (see page 310) or bought
   chicken stock
250ml coconut milk

We serve this at the Seafood Restaurant with the green bean and fresh coconut salad on page 315.

Cut the fish into 3–4cm chunks. Prepare the squid as shown on page 92. Peel the prawns as shown on page 68. Put the fish, squid and prawns into a shallow bowl and sprinkle with the salt, some pepper and the lime juice. Mix together well. Add half the spice paste and rub it well all over the pieces of seafood.

Heat the oil in a large pan over a medium heat. Add the remaining spice paste and fry gently for 2–3 minutes until it starts to smell fragrant. Add the kaffir lime leaves, lemongrass and stock and simmer for 1 minute.

Add the pieces of fish (not the squid or the prawns) to the pan and leave to cook for 1 minute, then turn them over and cook for a further minute. Add the coconut milk to the pan, together with the squid and prawns, and simmer for 2 minutes. Season to taste with a little more salt and lime juice and serve.

Crisp-fried fish Malaga-style

Alternative fish:
bream, flathead, grey
mullet, John Dory,
sand whiting, snapper

Olive oil, for deep-frying
Sea salt
Coarse flour such as harina
  de trigo especial para freir,
  or fine-ground semolina
Wedges of lemon, to serve

Amount per person
40g piece of red mullet fillet,
  pin-boned
1cm-thick, 60g steak of
  hake, whiting or sea bass,
  cut through the bone of
  a small fish
40g large, raw peeled prawns,
  with the last tail section
  of the shell still in place
  (see page 68)
40g squid (see page 92
  for squid preparation),
  cut into 5mm-thick rings

The seafront bars of southern Spain are known for their superb fried fish. Like Japanese tempura (see page 120), it's better to fry each person's fish individually.

Heat some oil for deep-frying to 190°C. Prepare the fish. Working with one person's portion of fish at a time, season each piece with salt and dredge in the flour.

Shake to remove excess flour, then drop into the hot oil and fry until crisp and golden. Cook the red mullet, hake or other fish and prawns for 30 seconds, then add the squid to the oil and cook them all for a further 30 seconds, by which time the fish should be cooked through.

Drain briefly on a baking tray lined with kitchen paper, then arrange on a warmed serving plate. Garnish with the lemon wedges and serve while it is still hot, then go on to cook the next portion.

Tempura of seafood

*Alternative fish:
flathead, flounder,
garfish, leatherjacket,
plaice, sand whiting*

SERVES 8
250g medium squid
    (pouches and tentacles)
20 raw tiger prawns
250g lemon sole fillet,
    skinned (see page 36)
Vegetable oil, for deep-frying

*For the soy and ginger
    dipping sauce*
90ml dark soy sauce
2 thin slices fresh ginger,
    finely chopped
Small bunch thin spring
    onions, finely sliced

*For the sweet chilli and
    five-spice dipping sauce*
150ml sweet chilli sauce
1 tbsp light soy sauce
¼ tsp Chinese five-spice
    powder
1½ tbsp cold water

For the batter
115g plain flour
115g cornflour
300ml ice-cold soda
    water, from a new bottle
Sea salt

I have picked up two vital tempura-making tips from Japanese chefs: first, to make the batter at the very last minute and hardly whisk it at all, and, second, to fry everything in small batches.

Prepare the squid as shown on page 92. Cut the pouches across into thin rings and separate the tentacles into pairs. Remove the heads of the prawns and peel them, leaving the last tail segment in place (see page 68). Skin the lemon sole fillet (see page 36), then cut across diagonally into strips about the thickness of your little finger.

Mix together the ingredients for the two dipping sauces and put into bowls for serving. Heat the oil for deep-frying to 190°C.

To make the batter, sift half the flour, half the cornflour and a pinch of salt into each of 2 large bowls. Stir 150ml of the ice-cold water into one bowl until just mixed. The batter should be a bit lumpy. If it seems thick, add a drop more water. You want the batter to coat the food in a thin, almost transparent layer.

Drop 8 pieces of mixed seafood into the batter, lift out one at a time and drop into the hot oil. Fry for 1 minute, then remove and drain on kitchen paper.

Serve with dipping sauces for eating straight away, while you make the next helping. Make a second batch of batter when you need it.

This recipe is for roughly 30 pieces, of which 24 will be nigiri sushi, and the last 6 nori sushi: rice wrapped in seaweed and containing keta (large salmon roe). It's a good idea to buy sushi-grade salmon and tuna fillet if you can find it.

Nigiri sushi

See technique on page 42.

Alternative fish:
albacore tuna, Arctic
char, bass, bream,
kingfish, ocean trout

SERVES 6
6 small raw unpeeled prawns
1 x 40–50g piece of thick
    tuna loin
1 x 40–50g thick piece
    of salmon fillet, skinned
    (see page 46)
1 x 40–50g lemon sole fillet,
    skinned (see page 36)
Wasabi paste
1 sheet nori
    (dried Japanese seaweed)
6 tsp keta

For the sticky rice
200g Japanese sticky rice
350ml cold water
2 tbsp rice vinegar
1 tbsp caster sugar
½ tsp salt

To serve
5 tbsp Tosa sauce
    (see page 312) or 4 tbsp
    Japanese dark soy sauce
    mixed with 1 tbsp mirin.
25g Japanese pickled ginger

First prepare the rice: put it into a large bowl, pour over cold water and run the grains through your fingers, changing the water now and then, until the water stays quite clear. Drain the rice and put it into a pan with the cold water. Bring to the boil, boil for 1 minute, then reduce the heat to low and simmer, covered, for 10 minutes. Remove from the heat and leave undisturbed for 10 minutes.

Meanwhile, gently heat the rice vinegar, sugar and salt in a small pan until the sugar has dissolved. Leave to cool.

Put the cooked rice into a bowl and fold in the vinegar mixture. Cover with cling film, but do not refrigerate.

To stop the prawns from curling when you cook them, push a cocktail stick or fine bamboo skewer just under the shell, from the head, along the under-belly, down to the tail. Drop them into lightly salted, boiling water and simmer for 3 minutes. Drain, drop them into cold water and leave to cool. Pull out the sticks, peel the prawns and then make a cut along the under-belly down to the tail, part-way into the flesh, so that you can open them out flat.

Cut the tuna and salmon into slices about 5mm thick; they should measures about 6 x 3cm. Cut the lemon sole into slices about 5mm, cutting on the diagonal to get as big a piece of fish as possible.

Mix a splash of rice vinegar with a cupful of cold water. Wet your hands with this, then mould 15g balls of the rice into small blocks, slightly smaller than the fish, without squashing the rice.

Smear one side of the tuna, lemon sole and salmon slices and the cut face of the prawns with a very small dot of wasabi paste. Lay each piece of fish and the prawns, wasabi-side down, on top of each block of rice and press down lightly.

Cut 5cm-wide strips of nori seaweed and wrap the last 6 blocks of rice in them, securing the seaweed with a dab of water. Place a spot of wasabi and a teaspoon of keta on to each.

To serve, divide the tosa sauce, or mixed soy sauce and mirin, between 6 dipping saucers. Serve the sushi with a little pile of pickled ginger and the sauce to the side.

Sashimi of salmon, tuna, sea bass and scallops

See technique on page 46.

Alternative fish:
albacore tuna, kingfish,
mahi mahi, ocean trout,
sable fish (black cod), shad,
snoek, yellowtail kingfish

SERVES 4

90g piece of salmon fillet,
  skinned and pin bones
  removed
90g piece of tuna fillet
90g piece of sea bass fillet,
  skinned and pin bones
  removed
4 scallops, out of the shell,
  corals removed
3 tbsp Tosa sauce
  (see page 312), to serve

For the garnish
7.5cm piece of daikon radish
  (mooli), peeled and finely
  shredded lengthways
Wasabi paste
20g Japanese pickled ginger

The size and shape of the fillets are important to the look of this dish. Buy 6cm-wide pieces of salmon and tuna loin. These you should cut into 5mm-thick slices. The sea bass should simply be cut as thinly as possible: this is because its texture is much firmer than of salmon and tuna. It's important to have a very sharp knife.

Carefully trim away the brown meat from the skinned side of the salmon fillet. Cut the salmon and tuna across into 5mm-thick slices. Cut the sea bass as thinly as possible, with your knife at 45 degrees. Cut each scallop horizontally into 3 slices.

Place 4 small heaps of daikon on each plate and arrange the fish on top. Put a hazelnut-sized amount of wasabi and a small pile of pickled ginger alongside, and serve the tosa sauce separately in a dipping saucer.

Empanada of seafood with tomatoes, peppers and pimentón

Alternative fish:
flathead, leatherjacket

MAKES 10-12
625g plain flour
1¼ tsp (7g) fast-action
    dried yeast
1¼ tsp (7g) salt
2 tsp (10g) pimentón dulce
    (smoked sweet paprika)
250ml hand-hot water
120ml olive oil
Lard or oil, for greasing
1 egg, beaten

For the filling
100ml olive oil
2 medium onions,
    finely chopped
3 garlic cloves, crushed
2 red peppers, seeded
    and chopped
2 tsp (10g) pimentón dulce
    (smoked sweet paprika)
2 x 400g cans chopped
    tomatoes
1 tsp salt
500g seafood: coley fillet,
    freshly filleted sardines,
    cooked octopus (see page
    94), all in 7–8cm strips;
    cooked mussel meats (see
    page 86), tinned tuna, prawns

Make the empanadas in baking trays using whatever seafood is to hand, layered with pimentón-flavoured tomato sauce. Pimentón goes into the crust, too, and adds a subtle flavour and a beautiful amber tint.

For the dough, sift the flour, yeast, salt and pimentón into a mixing bowl. Pour in the water along with the oil, and mix until everything comes together into a dough. Turn out on to a lightly floured surface and knead for 5 minutes until smooth. Put in a clean bowl, cover and leave somewhere warm for 1 hour.

For the filling, heat all but a tablespoon of the olive oil in a large, deep frying pan, add the onions, garlic, red peppers and pimentón and fry gently for about 25 minutes, stirring now and then, until soft and sweet. Add the tomatoes and salt and continue to cook gently for 35–40 minutes, stirring more frequently as the sauce gets thicker and is just starting to catch on the bottom of the pan.

Preheat the oven to 200°C/gas 6. Lightly grease a baking tray about 36 x 24cm and about 3cm deep with a little lard or oil.

Turn out the dough on to a lightly floured surface and knead once more until smooth. Cut in two, one piece slightly larger.

Cover the smaller piece and set to one side. Roll out the other piece and use to line the base and sides of the tin, leaving about 1cm overhanging.

Spoon half the tomato sauce into the tin and spread it over the pastry base. Season the fish and arrange it on top, then cover with the rest of the sauce. Sprinkle over the last tablespoon of olive oil. Roll out the remaining piece of dough into a rectangle the same size as the top of the tin. Lay it over the filling, brush the edge with beaten egg, then fold over the overhanging edges of dough and press them together to make a good seal. Pierce the top of the pie with a fork, brush with the beaten egg, and bake for 30 minutes or until richly golden.

Leave the empanada to rest for 10 minutes before cutting into pieces.

CHAPTER TWO

White fish

Hot pollack slices in a wrap with bok choi, beansprouts, garlic and ginger

Alternative fish:
any cheap, sustainable
fish, e.g. coley, hake,
leatherjacket, pollock,
whiting

SERVES 4

90g couscous
400g pollack fillet,
   cut into 1cm slices
Salt
90ml vegetable oil
15g (3 cloves) garlic, grated
15g fresh ginger, grated
4 Mexican-style flour tortilla
   wraps, 20cm in diameter
60g bok choi or salad
   cabbage, thinly sliced
60g beansprouts
8 spring onions, sliced
   on the diagonal
A small handful of
   coriander, roughly
   chopped
½ tsp Tabasco or
   Sriracha sauce
½ tsp soy sauce

Since I wrote my last *Seafood* book fourteen years ago, we've opened a couple of fish and chip restaurants and this seafood wrap is a great favourite. I particularly like the crunchy texture from the couscous.

Put the couscous in a shallow bowl. Season the fish lightly with salt and turn over in the couscous, then gently fry in a shallow pan with the vegetable oil for 3 minutes. Remove the fish to a plate, add the garlic and ginger to the pan and fry with the residual couscous for 1–2 minutes.

To warm the tortillas, place on a hot, dry frying pan or under a hot grill for approximately 6 seconds on each side.

Place the fish in the centre of each of the wraps. Sprinkle with bok choi and beansprouts, then spoon over the garlic, ginger, couscous and oil from the pan. Cover with the spring onions and coriander, then drizzle over the Tabasco and soy sauce. Fold up the wraps and serve.

Cod with Puy lentils and red wine sauce

Alternative fish: barramundi, blue cod, blue-eye trevalla, coley, haddock, hake, hapuka, murray cod, pollock

SERVES 4

75g unsalted butter
4 x 175g pieces of thick
    skin-on cod fillet
    (see page 22)
Coarse sea salt and freshly
    ground black pepper
50g each onion, carrot and
    celery, finely chopped
A small pinch each of ground
    allspice, ground cloves
    and grated nutmeg
A large pinch of curry powder
600ml red wine
600ml Chicken stock
    (see page 310)
1 tsp sugar
¼ tsp salt
1 tbsp plain flour

For the lentils
50g dried Puy lentils
300ml Fish stock
    (see page 310)
1 clove and 1 bay leaf
2 slices peeled onion
½ tsp salt

This is a very early dish from the Seafood Restaurant, which we still feature. I wrote it with memories of French restaurants, where Asian spices are used pleasingly in a sotto voce manner in butter sauces.

Put all the ingredients for the lentils into a pan and simmer until tender. Drain, then cover and keep warm.

Melt 50g of the butter in a medium pan and brush a little all over the cod. Season the fish on both sides and put skin-side up on a baking tray.

For the sauce, add the chopped onion, carrot and celery and spices to the melted butter in the pan and fry over a medium heat for about 10 minutes. Add the red wine, stock, sugar and salt, bring to the boil and boil until the sauce is reduced by three-quarters and is concentrated in flavour. Strain into a clean pan and keep warm.

Preheat the grill to high. Grill the cod for 8 minutes, until the skin is well browned. Mix the remaining 25g butter with the flour to make a smooth paste (beurre manié). Bring the sauce to the boil and then whisk in the paste, a little at a time. Simmer for 2 minutes until smooth and thickened.

To serve, spoon the lentils on to 4 warmed plates and place the cod on top. Spoon the sauce around the edge.

Salt cod, chickpea and spinach stew

Alternative fish:
salted blue cod, salted
blue-eye trevalla, salted
flathead, salted pollock

SERVES 4

350g dried chickpeas, soaked
    for 24 hours and drained
1 small head of garlic,
    loose skin removed
2 medium onions, chopped
3 fresh bay leaves
100ml olive oil
350g fresh salted cod or
    half the amount of bought
    salt cod, soaked and
    drained (see page 67)
3–4 garlic cloves, finely
    chopped
A good pinch of crushed
    dried chillies
1 tsp pimentón picante
    (smoked hot Spanish
    paprika)
3 medium or 400g tin
    tomatoes, chopped
½ tsp loosely packed
    saffron strands
250g spinach leaves,
    torn up if large
Salt

To serve
4–6 tbsp Aïoli (see page 311)
Crusty fresh bread

This salt cod and chickpea stew is distinctly Spanish in its use of pimentón. If using bought salt cod (bacalao), soak it in 3–4 litres of water in the fridge for 24–48 hours, changing the water when it tastes salty – at least twice.

Put the drained chickpeas into a large pan with the head of garlic, half the chopped onion, the bay leaves, 50ml of the olive oil and 2 litres of cold water. Bring to the boil, then lower the heat and leave to simmer for 1½ hours or until the chickpeas are just tender.

Barely cover the salt cod with water in a pan and simmer for 8 minutes until just cooked through. Remove the fish and break into large flakes, discarding the skin and any bones. Reserve the cooking water.

Heat 3 tablespoons of the oil in a frying pan over a medium heat. Add the remaining onion, the chopped garlic, chilli flakes and pimentón and fry for 6–7 minutes until soft and lightly golden. Add the tomatoes and cook for another 10 minutes into a thick sauce.

Remove and discard the bay leaves from the chickpeas. Lift out the garlic and squeeze the pulp back into the pan. Stir in the tomato mixture with the saffron, and a little of the salt-cod cooking liquid if the mixture is too thick, and simmer for 15 minutes more.

Add the spinach and cook for 2 minutes. Stir in the salt cod, check the seasoning and add salt to taste. Serve in shallow bowls, with a drizzle of oil, a dollop of the aïoli and some crusty bread.

Brandade de morue

Alternative fish:
any of the following,
fresh salted – blue cod,
coley, dhufish, haddock,
hake, hoki, pollock

SERVES 4-6
12 thin slices of baguette,
    cut on the diagonal
150ml olive oil
500g fresh salted cod or half
    the amount of bought salt
    cod, soaked (see page 67)
3 garlic cloves, crushed
175ml double cream
Lemon juice
Freshly ground black pepper

To garnish
Black olives
Chopped flat-leaf parsley

I sometimes have a double portion of this as a main course. It's a sort of fish fondue, and I like lots of crusty bread as well as the fried bread, and a glass or two of Beaujolais.

Fry the bread in 2 tablespoons of the olive oil for a minute or two on either side until golden brown. Drain briefly on kitchen paper and keep warm in a low oven.

Drain the soaked salted cod. Put it into a pan with enough fresh water to barely cover, bring to the boil and simmer for 7 minutes. Drain, then remove any skin and bones.

Put the garlic, the remaining olive oil and the cream into a small pan and bring to the boil. Pour into a food processor with the fish and blend together until just smooth. Season to taste with lemon juice and plenty of black pepper. No salt should be needed.

Serve warm garnished with black olives and parsley with the fried bread alongside.

Fish burger with red onion, lettuce, tomato and chipotle relish

SERVES 4

60g flour
1 egg
60g panko breadcrumbs
400g fish, cut in
    1cm-thick slices
Salt
150ml vegetable oil,
    for frying
4 hamburger buns
60g little gem or iceberg
    lettuce, sliced
150g tomato, thinly sliced
60g red onion, thinly sliced
60g Mayonnaise (see page 311)
    or Japanese Kewpie
    mayonnaise
60ml Chipotle relish
    (see page 312) or a favourite
    brand of chilli tomato relish
1 fresh red chilli, thinly sliced

This burger is very popular at our chippies. The type of fish in it doesn't really matter – use whatever is cheap. It is well worth making the chipotle relish. It's very good with fried eggs too.

Put the flour, egg and breadcrumbs in 3 shallow dishes. Season the fish with salt and put in the flour, then egg, then breadcrumbs. Shallow-fry the fish in the oil over a medium heat until the breadcrumbs are light brown and crisp: about 1½ minutes each side.

Cut the buns in half and assemble the burger. Start with the lettuce, then the tomato and onion, then the mayonnaise and the relish. Finally rest the fish on top, sprinkle with fresh chilli, top with the other half of the bun and serve.

Hake with clams, asparagus, peas and parsley

Alternative fish: blue-eye trevalla, haddock, John Dory, mahi mahi, monkfish

SERVES 4

4 x 175–200g pieces of skinned hake fillet, cut about 2cm thick
Salt
200g asparagus tips, each about 8cm long
250g fresh or frozen peas
Plain flour, for dusting, plus 1 tbsp
6 tbsp olive oil
4 garlic cloves, finely chopped
100g finely chopped shallot
1 tbsp flour
175ml dry white wine
100ml Fish stock (see page 310)
250g small clams, such as carpetshell, washed
1 tbsp chopped flat-leaf parsley leaves

The asparagus for this traditional Basque dish would normally be white, but as it's hard to get fresh white asparagus in the UK, I make it with green instead.

Season the pieces of hake generously on both sides with salt and set aside for 10–15 minutes. Wash in cold water and pat dry.

Cook the asparagus tips in well-salted water for 2 minutes, then add the peas, bring back to the boil, drain and refresh under cold running water. Leave to drain.

Dust the hake pieces in flour and shake off the excess. Heat 4 tablespoons of the olive oil in a large frying pan over a medium-high heat. Add the hake and fry for 2–3 minutes on each side until golden brown on the outside but not quite cooked through. Lift out on to a plate and set to one side; wipe the pan clean.

Add the remaining 2 tablespoons oil and the garlic and shallot to the pan and fry over a medium heat for 3 minutes or until soft and lightly golden. Stir in the tablespoon of flour, then gradually stir in the wine and stock to make a smooth sauce. Bring to a simmer, return the hake to the pan and cook for 1 minute. Add the clams, cover and cook for 2–3 minutes until all the clams have opened and the fish is cooked through. Uncover and scatter over the asparagus tips, peas and parsley. Simmer for a minute or two more until the vegetables have heated through, and serve.

Hake en papillote with oven-roasted tomatoes and tapenade

See technique on page 60.

Alternative fish:
any thick fillets of good-sized fish such as cod, haddock, salmon and even large sea bass, or other grouper-type fish, such as blue-eye trevalla, blue cod, hapuka, kinglip and mahi mahi

SERVES 4

Olive oil, for brushing
2 tbsp finely shredded
   basil leaves
4 x 200g pieces of thick
   skin-on hake fillet
Salt and freshly ground
   black pepper
4 tbsp Tapenade
   (see page 312)

For the oven-roasted tomatoes
750g ripe plum tomatoes
½ tsp sea salt flakes
1 tsp thyme leaves

Cooking fish in a paper parcel is a great idea for two reasons: one, the flavours get trapped inside, and two, it's perfect for having friends around because the fiddly preparation can be done ahead.

Preheat the oven to 240°C/gas 9. Cut the tomatoes in half and place cut-side up in a lightly oiled roasting tin. Sprinkle over the sea salt, thyme and some pepper and roast for 15 minutes. Lower the temperature to 150°C/gas 2 and roast for a further 1½ hours until shrivelled to about half their original size. Remove and leave to cool. This can be done in advance.

Return the oven temperature to 240°C/gas 9. Prepare the paper and foil squares as described on page 60. Put 3 pieces of tomato slightly off-centre on each square and sprinkle over the basil. Season the pieces of hake on both sides with salt and pepper and put them on top of the tomatoes. Seal the parcels, place on a baking sheet and bake for 15 minutes.

Serve the papillotes on a large plate, with tapenade in a bowl on the side, and slit the parcels open at the table so that everyone can enjoy the aroma.

Grilled hake on spring onion mash with soy butter

Alternative fish:
hapuka, John Dory,
mahi mahi, Pacific
halibut, pollock, snapper

SERVES 4

4 x 200g pieces of skin-on
  thick hake fillet
A little melted butter,
  for brushing
1 tsp salt
Sea salt flakes and coarsely
  crushed black pepper

For the spring onion mash
1.25kg Maris Piper or other
  floury potatoes, peeled
  and cut into chunks
50g butter
1 bunch spring onions,
  thinly sliced
A little milk
Salt and freshly ground
  white pepper

For the soy butter sauce
600ml Chicken stock
  (see page 310)
2 tbsp dark soy sauce
75g unsalted butter
1 tomato, skinned,
  seeded and diced
1 heaped tsp chopped
  coriander

Still popular on our St Petroc's Bistro menu.
The combination of chicken stock, butter, soy sauce,
tomato and coriander with the hake is irresistible.

Put the fish, skin-side down, in a shallow dish and sprinkle
with the salt. Set aside for 30 minutes. Then rinse the salt off
and dry the fish on kitchen paper. Brush each piece with melted
butter and put skin-side up on a greased baking tray. Sprinkle
the skin with a few sea salt flakes and some black pepper.

For the spring onion mash, cook the potatoes in boiling
unsalted water for 20 minutes until tender.

For the sauce, put the chicken stock and soy sauce into
another pan and boil rapidly until it has reduced by half.

Preheat the grill to high. Grill the hake for 8 minutes on
one side only.

Just before the fish is ready, add the butter to the sauce
and whisk it in. Remove from the heat and add the tomato
and coriander.

Drain the potatoes, return to the pan and mash until
smooth. Heat the butter in another pan, add the spring onions
and turn them over in the butter for a few seconds. Beat them
into the potato with a little milk and some salt and white pepper.
Spoon the spring onion mash into the centre of 4 warmed plates.
Rest the hake on top and spoon the sauce around the outside.

Braised ling with lettuce, peas and crisp smoked pancetta

Alternative fish:
Dover sole, flathead,
John Dory, leatherjacket,
mahi mahi, monkfish

SERVES 4

4 x 200g pieces of thick
ling fillet, skinned
100ml Chicken stock
(see page 310)
100g butter
12 large salad onions,
trimmed and cut into
2cm pieces
4 little gem lettuce hearts,
cut into quarters
350g fresh or frozen peas
8 very thin slices smoked
pancetta or rindless
smoked streaky bacon
1 tbsp chopped chervil
or parsley
Salt and freshly ground
white pepper

I wrote this recipe for ling as it has the quality of being very firm-textured, and was and still is quite a reasonably priced member of the cod family, but the dish works equally well with other firm-fleshed fish such as monkfish or John Dory.

Season the pieces of ling with some salt. Bring the chicken stock to the boil in a small pan and keep hot.

Melt half the butter in a wide shallow casserole dish, add the onions and cook gently for 2–3 minutes, until tender but not browned. Add the lettuce and turn over once or twice in the butter. Add the peas, hot chicken stock and some salt and pepper and simmer rapidly for 3–4 minutes, turning the lettuce hearts now and then, until the vegetables have started to soften and about three-quarters of the liquid has evaporated. Put the pieces of ling on top of the vegetables, then cover and simmer for 7–8 minutes, until the fish is cooked through.

Shortly before the fish is cooked, heat a ridged cast-iron griddle over a high heat and grill the pancetta or bacon for about 1 minute on each side, until crisp and golden. Keep warm.

Uncover the casserole dish, dot the remaining butter around the pan and sprinkle the chopped chervil or parsley over the vegetables. Shake the pan over the heat until the butter has melted and amalgamated with the cooking juices to make a sauce. Garnish the fish with the grilled pancetta and serve.

Haddock a la plancha with caramelized garlic

Alternative fish:
barramundi, bass,
blue-eye trevalla,
hake, murray cod,
sable fish (black cod),
snapper, toothfish

SERVES 2
4 x 100–125g skin-on
   haddock fillets
Salt
2 tbsp olive oil
2 tbsp Slow-cooked
   garlic (see page 312)

'A la plancha' means cooked on a thick steel griddle. Any large frying pan makes a good substitute. I found this dish in Galicia, northern Spain, where they cook a lot of fish this way. The method is perfect for small Cornish haddock, but fillets of larger fish are easier to get hold of so I've based the recipe around those.

Season the fish fillets on both sides with a little salt. Heat a large frying pan over a high heat. Add the olive oil and as soon as it is shimmering hot, add the fish, flesh-side down first, and cook for 2 minutes, until richly golden. Turn the fish over and cook for 1 more minute. Carefully remove the fish from the pan, remove the pan from the heat and leave it to cool very slightly. If you add the garlic to the pan straight away it will burn.

Return the pan to a medium heat, add the slow-cooked garlic and cook until it is just golden brown. Return the fish fillets to the pan, flesh-side down, and shake around briefly to encourage the garlic to stick to the fish. Remove from the pan once more and serve flesh-side up with any remaining garlic from the pan spooned over.

Mild potato curry topped with smoked haddock and a poached egg

SERVES 4

4 x 100g pieces of
  smoked haddock fillet
2 tsp white wine vinegar
4 eggs
Sprigs of coriander,
  to garnish

For the potato curry

700g waxy main-crop
  potatoes, peeled and
  cut into 1cm dice
4 tbsp sunflower oil
1 tsp yellow mustard seeds
200g onions, finely chopped
½ tsp turmeric powder
4 tomatoes, skinned
  and chopped
2 tsp roughly chopped
  coriander
Salt and freshly ground
  black pepper

There's no real alternative to smoked haddock, but you could do your own with any thick fillet of white fish brined (see page 203) and smoked (see the technique on page 64).

For the potato curry, cook the potatoes in boiling salted water for 6–7 minutes until tender, then drain. Meanwhile, heat the oil in a pan, add the mustard seeds and, when they begin to pop, add the onions. Fry for 7–8 minutes or until the onions are soft and lightly browned. Add the turmeric and potatoes and some salt and pepper and fry for 1–2 minutes. Add the tomatoes and cook for 1 minute. Stir in the chopped coriander, set aside and keep warm.

Bring about 5cm water to the boil in a shallow pan. Add the pieces of smoked haddock, bring back to a simmer and poach for 4 minutes. Lift out with a slotted spoon, cover and keep warm.

Discard the fish poaching liquor, pour another 5cm water into the pan and bring to a very gentle simmer; the water should be just trembling and there should be a few bubbles rising up from the bottom of the pan. Add the vinegar, break in the eggs and poach for 3 minutes. Lift out with a slotted spoon and drain briefly on kitchen paper.

To serve, spoon the potato curry into the centre of 4 warmed plates. Skin the haddock and put on top of the potatoes. Put a poached egg on top of the fish and garnish with the sprigs of coriander.

Merlan frit en colère (deep-fried whiting)

See technique on page 30.

Alternative fish:
pin hake, sand whiting
or any small (up to 500g)
white fish

SERVES 4
4 x 350g whiting, cleaned
   and trimmed (see page 16)
Sunflower oil, for deep-frying
75g plain flour
Salt and freshly ground
   black pepper
2 eggs, beaten
175g fresh white breadcrumbs,
   made from day-old bread, or
   Japanese panko breadcrumbs
Chunky chips, to serve

For the tomato tartare sauce
3 tbsp white wine vinegar
6 black peppercorns,
   coarsely crushed
½ shallot, finely chopped
A few tarragon stalks,
   broken into small pieces
2 plum tomatoes, skinned,
   seeded and finely chopped
15g each green olives, gherkins
   and capers, finely chopped
2 tsp each tarragon, parsley
   and chives, chopped
100g Mustard mayonnaise
   (see page 311)

I've always liked the name of this dish, which means something like 'whiting in a bad temper'. The whiting's tail is twisted round and secured in its mouth before being breaded and deep-fried.

For the sauce, put the vinegar, peppercorns, shallot and tarragon stalks into a small pan and boil until the vinegar is reduced to 1 tsp. Cool slightly then strain into a bowl. Mix in the rest of the ingredients and some salt and pepper.

Prepare the whiting for cooking as described on page 30. Heat some oil for deep-frying to 160°C. Season the flour with ½ teaspoon of salt and some pepper. Season each fish with a little salt, then coat them one at a time in the flour, followed by the beaten egg and then the breadcrumbs.

Deep-fry the fish for 5 minutes or until crisp and golden and cooked through. Transfer to a baking tray lined with kitchen paper and keep warm in a low oven while you coat and cook the rest of the fish. Serve with the tomato tartare sauce and some chunky chips.

Steamed grey mullet with garlic, ginger and spring onions

Alternative fish:
bass, bream, carp, snapper

SERVES 2

2 x 500g grey mullet,
    cleaned and trimmed
    (see page 16, steps 1–4)
2.5cm fresh ginger,
    cut into matchsticks
8 spring onions, trimmed
    and finely shredded
2 tbsp dark soy sauce
2 tbsp sesame oil
4 garlic cloves,
    finely chopped

Steaming fish with ginger and serving it with soy sauce and spring onions is a classic Chinese treatment that never fails to hit the spot.

Put the fish into a steamer and sprinkle over the ginger. Cover and steam for 10–12 minutes until cooked through. Lift the fish on to 2 warmed serving plates, scatter over the spring onions and keep warm.

Pour 4 tablespoons of the cooking juices into a small pan and add the soy sauce. Bring up to the boil and pour over the fish.

Heat the sesame oil in a small pan. Add the garlic, fry for a few seconds, then pour over the fish and serve.

Grey mullet soup with harissa, spring onions and pink fir apple potatoes

*Alternative fish:
any kind of medium-oily
fish, such as red mullet,
sea bass, snapper*

SERVES 4

1kg whole grey mullet
90ml olive oil
1 medium onion, sliced
1 carrot, sliced
1 stick celery, sliced
½ garlic bulb, sliced but
  not peeled
2 tbsp Harissa (see page 312)
  or a brand such as Harissa
  du Cap-Bon
400g chopped tomatoes,
  fresh or canned
2 tbsp tomato purée
A pinch of saffron threads,
  if using commercial harissa
Piece of orange peel
1 tsp salt
1.5 litres water
300g pink fir apple potatoes
  or other small waxy potatoes,
  peeled and sliced lengthways
10 spring onions, sliced on
  the diagonal
A small handful of parsley,
  finely chopped
1 quantity Aïoli (see page 311)

Although I've called this a soup, it's more like fish with sauce, albeit lots of it. The soup can be made with commercial harissa, but add saffron in that case.

Scale, gut and fillet the fish (see pages 16 and 20). Cut the fillet into 2cm-wide slices.

Use the head and bones to make a stock: heat half the olive oil in a pan. Add the onion, carrot, celery and garlic and all the fish trimmings. Fry for 5 minutes, stirring constantly. Add half the harissa, the tomatoes, tomato purée, saffron (if using), orange peel, salt and water.

Bring to the boil and simmer for half an hour. Pass through a fine strainer, pressing through as much of the stock using the back of a ladle as possible. Discard the solids. Return the stock to the heat and reduce by half.

Boil the potatoes in salted water until tender.

Heat a frying pan with the remaining olive oil and cook the fillets skin-side down over a moderate heat for 6–7 minutes.

Put the mullet, potatoes and spring onions into 4 warmed, wide soup bowls, sprinkle on the parsley, pour the soup gently on top and add a dollop of aïoli.

A fillet of John Dory with white crab and asparagus

Alternative fish:
bream, flathead, galjoen,
mullet, rock cod, snapper

SERVES 4 AS A
FIRST COURSE
500g small unpeeled prawns
2 tbsp olive oil
1 medium onion, chopped
1 carrot, chopped
2 garlic cloves, chopped
800ml Fish stock
  (see page 310)
100g fresh thin asparagus
350g skin-on John Dory fillets
100g unsalted butter,
  chilled, cut into pieces
Salt and freshly ground
  black pepper
200ml double cream
1 tbsp lemon juice
200g white crab meat

A fragrant dish rich with prawns and crab meat, which is considered old-fashioned but goes ever so well with a white burgundy.

For the stock, peel the prawns (see page 68), keeping the shells. Heat the olive oil in a pan. Add the shells, onion, carrot and garlic and fry gently for 6–7 minutes until soft and lightly browned. Add the fish stock, cover and simmer for 40 minutes. Pass through a fine strainer into a clean, wide-based pan, pressing out as much liquid as you can from the shells using the back of a ladle.

Cut the asparagus into 10cm lengths, briefly cook in salted water and drain.

Cut the John Dory fillets into 2 pieces along the natural break. Melt a little of the butter and brush it over the fish, and season lightly with salt and pepper. Place, skin-side up, on a lightly buttered baking tray ready to grill; preheat the grill to high.

Boil the prawn-flavoured stock until reduced by half. Add the double cream and boil rapidly until reduced once more by about half. Whisk in the butter pieces, 2–3 at a time, then stir in the lemon juice and salt to taste.

Grill the John Dory for 4 minutes until just cooked through. Meanwhile, stir the prawns into the sauce and cook for about 1 minute. Add the crab meat and asparagus and heat through. Serve with the grilled fillets on 4 warm plates.

Roasted gurnard with a Thai hot, sour and sweet sauce

Alternative fish:
John Dory, sea bass,
sea bream, silver perch,
snapper, tilapia, whiting

SERVES 4

4 gurnard, each weighing
   about 300–400g,
   scaled and trimmed
75ml fish sauce, plus
   extra if needed
Vegetable oil
50g shallots, thinly sliced
25g garlic, thinly sliced
3 red bird's-eye chillies,
   thinly sliced
50g palm sugar
30g piece of seedless
   tamarind pulp
4 tbsp water

Instead of roasting, you could also barbecue or grill the fish, or even deep-fry it at 190°C for 5–6 minutes until crisp and golden. Serve it with steamed bok choi and Thai jasmine rice.

Preheat the oven to 220°C/gas 7. Make 3 slashes on either side of each fish and place in a shallow dish. Pour over the fish sauce and work it into the slashes and the belly cavity. Pour the excess off into a small pan. You should be left with about 50ml but, if not, make up to this amount.

Set the fish to one side while you make the sauce. Heat 1cm oil in a medium frying pan over a medium-high heat. Add the shallots and fry them, stirring now and then, until crisp and golden. Lift out on to kitchen paper and leave to drain. Add the sliced garlic to the oil and fry until crisp and golden. Lift out and leave to cool and drain alongside the shallots. Add the sliced chillies and fry for a few seconds until lightly golden. Remove and leave to drain too.

Add the sugar, tamarind pulp and water to the small pan containing the fish sauce. Bring to the boil, stirring to break up the pulp, and simmer for about 1 minute until thickened. Pass through a sieve into a bowl, pressing out as much liquid as you can. Return to a clean pan and set aside.

Transfer the fish to a lightly oiled roasting tin and roast for 12 minutes or until the flesh at the thickest part, just behind the head, is opaque and comes away from the bones easily. It should register 57–60°C on a thermal probe. Bring the sauce back to a gentle simmer and stir in half the fried shallots, garlic and chilli. Serve the fish with some of the sauce spooned over, and scattered with the remaining fried shallots, garlic and chilli.

Poached quenelles of gurnard with prawn sauce

See technique on page 62.

Alternative fish:
black bream, blue fish (tailor),
coley, flathead, grey mullet,
leatherjacket, megrim sole

SERVES 4
25g butter, melted
150ml milk
50g fresh white breadcrumbs
350g gurnard fillets,
    skinned and boned
A pinch of freshly grated
    nutmeg
2 tsp lemon juice
1 egg
Salt and freshly ground
    white pepper
125ml double cream

For the prawn sauce
1 quantity Shellfish
    reduction (see page 310),
    made with prawns
90ml double cream
1 tsp Beurre manié
    (see page 311)
1 egg yolk

Gurnard makes a good quenelle – fish mousse, moulded into oval shapes and poached in water – because of its firm texture and robust flavour. Use ingredients straight from the fridge for the best results.

Mix the butter, milk and breadcrumbs into a coarse paste. Cover and chill for 30 minutes. Cut the gurnard fillets into small pieces and put into a food processor with the breadcrumb paste, nutmeg, lemon juice, egg and seasoning. Blend for at least 1 minute to a very fine paste. Transfer the mixture to a large bowl sitting inside a bowl of iced water. Add the cream a little at a time, beating between each addition, so the mixture becomes light and thickens. Cover and chill for 30 minutes.

For the sauce, heat the shellfish reduction in a small pan. Add half the cream and the beurre manié and whisk over a medium heat for a few minutes until smooth and thickened. Keep warm.

Mould and cook the quenelles as described on page 62, then divide between 4 individual dishes or 1 large gratin dish. Preheat the grill to very high.

Whisk together the egg yolk and remaining cream and stir it into the sauce. Stir over a low heat until thickened, but not boiling. Pour over the quenelles and grill for about a minute until lightly browned.

Pan-fried gurnard with sage and garlic butter

See technique on page 28.

Alternative fish:
bass, bream, flathead,
John Dory, kinglip,
red mullet, sand
whiting, snapper

SERVES 4
4 x 350–450g gurnard
4 tsp sunflower oil
75g unsalted butter
2 garlic cloves,
    finely chopped
2 tbsp small sage leaves
2 tbsp lemon juice
Salt and freshly ground
    black pepper

If you find the technique for skinning a whole gurnard a little tricky, this dish would work equally well with fillets.

Skin the whole gurnard as described on page 28, then season on both sides with some salt and pepper.

Heat the oil in a large frying pan. Add the fish and 15g of the butter and fry over a medium-high heat for about 4 minutes on each side until golden brown. Lift out and keep warm.

Wipe out the pan with kitchen paper. Add the rest of the butter and, as it starts to melt, add the garlic and sage leaves. Return the pan to the heat and leave the butter to cook gently for about 30 seconds. Quickly add the lemon juice and some seasoning, then serve the fish with the sauce spooned over.

Whole sea bass baked with red peppers, tomatoes, anchovies and potatoes

See technique on page 56.

*Alternative fish:
any slightly oily fish
such as barramundi,
bream, coral trout,
gurnard, snapper
and striped bass*

SERVES 4

A good pinch of
  saffron strands
1kg waxy potatoes, peeled
  and cut into 1cm slices
4 plum tomatoes, skinned and
  cut lengthways into quarters
50g anchovy fillets in oil,
  drained
150ml Chicken stock
  (see page 310)
4 red peppers, each one seeded
  and cut into 8 chunks
8 garlic cloves,
  each sliced into 3
8 small sprigs oregano
90ml olive oil
1 x 1.5–1.75g sea bass,
  cleaned and trimmed
  (see page 16)
Salt and freshly ground
  black pepper

I roast all the vegetables before adding the sea bass simply because fish cooks so quickly. A temperature probe is useful here.

Preheat the oven to 200°C/gas 6. Soak the saffron in 2 tablespoons of hot water.

Par-boil the potatoes in boiling salted water for 7 minutes. Drain well and arrange them in the roasting dish to form a bed for the fish, leaving plenty of room on either side for the red peppers.

Scatter the tomatoes and anchovy fillets over the potatoes, then pour over the saffron water and stock. Scatter the pieces of red pepper alongside the potatoes and sprinkle over the garlic, oregano sprigs and olive oil. Season everything well and bake for 30 minutes.

Slash the fish 5–6 times down each side then slash it in the opposite direction on just one side to give an attractive criss-cross pattern. Rub it generously with some olive oil, season well and rest it on top of the potatoes. Return the dish to the oven and bake for a further 35 minutes until the fish is cooked through: the temperature next to the backbone should be about 57–60°C. Serve with the roasted vegetables.

Sea bass baked in a salt crust with a lemon sauce and a potato, tomato and basil confit

See technique on page 58.

Alternative fish:
bream, flathead, galjoen,
grey mullet, gurnard, John
Dory, mussel cracker, red
mullet, sea trout, shad, silver
perch, snapper, warehou

SERVES 4
2 x 750g sea bass, gutted
   (see page 16)
1.75kg cooking salt
2 egg whites

For the lemon sauce
600ml Fish stock
   (see page 310)
1 tsp fennel seeds
½ small lemon, sliced
120ml dry white wine
½ tsp salt
2 egg yolks
200ml olive oil, warmed

For the confit
50ml olive oil
1 small onion, finely chopped
1 garlic clove, finely chopped
500g waxy new potatoes,
   peeled and cut into quarters
1 beefsteak tomato or 2 large
   plum tomatoes, chopped
½ tsp salt
2 tbsp finely shredded basil

It took us a long time to adopt cooking a whole fish in a salt crust at the Seafood Restaurant because once it was in the crust it was impossible to tell if it was cooked. Now, using a temperature probe, it's no problem. The temperature should be 55 to 60°C.

Preheat the oven to 200°C/gas 6. For the sauce, put the fish stock, fennel seeds, sliced lemon, white wine and salt into a pan and boil rapidly until the liquid has reduced to about 4 tablespoons. Strain into a small bowl and leave to cool. Put the egg yolks and reduced stock mixture into a liquidizer. With the motor running, gradually pour in the oil to make a thick, mayonnaise-like mixture. Transfer to a bowl and season to taste.

For the potato confit, heat the olive oil in a pan, add the onion and garlic and sauté for 5–10 minutes over a moderate heat. Add the potatoes, tomato and salt and cook gently for 25 minutes. Stir in the basil.

While the potatoes are cooking, prepare the sea bass. Mix the salt with the egg whites, then follow the instructions on page 58. Bake the fish in the salt crust for 20 minutes or until they reach 57–60°C inside. Remove from the oven, lift away the crust, skin the fish and lift off the fillets.

Serve the potato, tomato and basil confit alongside the fillets of fish together with the lemon sauce.

Grilled whole sea bass with Pernod and fennel

*Alternative fish:
bream, coral trout,
dhufish, flathead,
grey mullet, gurnard,
John Dory, monkfish,
morwong, mussel cracker,
red emperor, red mullet,
shad, snapper, tarakihi*

SERVES 4
4 x 450–550g sea bass,
    cleaned and trimmed
    (see page 16)
2 tbsp olive oil
Salt and freshly ground
    black pepper
1 large bunch fennel herb
3 tbsp Pernod
1 quantity Fennel mayonnaise
    (see page 311)

Sea bass seems to have an affinity with the flavours of fennel and anise. If you intend to barbecue the fish, and don't plan to eat the skin, leave the fish scales on to stop it sticking to the grill bars. You need a temperature probe to judge exactly when the fish is done.

Slash each fish 4 or 5 times down each side (see page 17). Rub with the oil and season outside and inside the gut cavities well. Push some of the fennel herb into the gut cavity of each fish. If barbecuing, it's a good idea to put the fish into a wire clamp. If you are not barbecuing, preheat the grill to hot.

Barbecue or grill the fish for 6–8 minutes. Sprinkle each one with about 1 teaspoon of Pernod, carefully turn over and cook for another 6–8 minutes. The centre of the fish should be 57–60°C. Sprinkle with the rest of the Pernod.

Lift the fish on to a warmed serving plate and serve with the fennel mayonnaise.

What makes this Malaysian soup particularly good is its base of intense laksa 'gravy': spiced, soured fish stock flavoured with galangal, chillies, shrimp paste, tamarind, sugar and Vietnamese mint (*Persicaria odorata*).

Penang Road laksa

Alternative fish:
barramundi, coral trout,
flathead, flounder, galjoen,
John Dory, red mullet, whiting

SERVES 4

2 x 350g sea bass or snapper
2 fat lemongrass stalks, bruised
1 tsp salt
1 quantity Penang laksa spice
  paste (see page 314)
1 quantity Tamarind water
  (see page 312)
3 tbsp fish sauce
2 tsp palm sugar
300g fresh round rice noodles
  or 175g dried 5mm-wide
  flat rice noodles (banh pho)

For the toppings
¼ cucumber, cut into
  long thin strips
Small wedge of fresh
  pineapple, cut into
  long thin strips
1 small crisp lettuce, sliced
  across into 1cm-wide strips
100g shallots or 1 small red
  onion, thinly sliced
2 red bird's-eye chillies, sliced
A handful of mint leaves,
  such as Vietnamese

Clean, scale and trim the fish as shown on page 16. Bring 1.5 litres of water to the boil in a large pan. Add the fish, lemongrass and salt, bring back to a simmer and cook the fish for just 10 minutes. Then lift on to a plate and leave to cool slightly.

Add the spice paste, tamarind water, fish sauce and sugar to the pan, cover and simmer for 30 minutes. Strain the laksa 'gravy' through a sieve into a bowl, pressing out as much flavour as you can, then return to a clean pan, bring back to a simmer and keep hot. Meanwhile, flake the flesh from the fish, discarding bones and skin.

Arrange the fish and all the topping ingredients on a serving plate.

Bring a pan of unsalted water to the boil. If using dried noodles, soak them in unsalted boiling water for 3–4 minutes or until just tender, then drain. If using fresh noodles, drop them into boiling water, leave for a few seconds to heat through, then drain.

Divide the noodles between 4 bowls and ladle over the hot laksa 'gravy'. Invite your guests to add their desired toppings and some flaked fish.

Sea bass pollichathu in banana leaf

Alternative fish:
bream, dab, John Dory,
plaice, flounder, grunter,
lemon sole, luderick, sand
whiting, snapper, tilapia

SERVES 4
4 whole sea bass,
   each weighing about
   250–300g, gutted and
   trimmed (see page 16)
2 tbsp coconut oil or
   vegetable oil, for frying

For the marinade
2 tbsp lemon juice
1 tsp salt
½ tsp turmeric powder
½ tsp Kashmiri chilli powder

For the masala
50ml coconut oil
   or vegetable oil
1 small onion, finely sliced
1 small tomato, finely sliced
1 tsp ground black pepper
1 tsp Garam masala
   (see page 314)
1 tsp Kashmiri chilli powder
½ tsp turmeric powder
1 tsp salt
A handful of fresh curry leaves
2 green chillies, finely
   chopped, with seeds

This recipe was cooked for me at a waterside restaurant I discovered while exploring the Backwaters of Alleppey, in Kerala, southern India. I've written the recipe for the fish to be steamed in foil, but do use banana leaves if you can get them, as this is what makes the dish a true pollichathu.

Mix together the marinade ingredients in a shallow dish, add the fish and turn to coat. Set aside while you make the masala.

For the masala, heat the oil in a heavy-based pan over a medium heat. Add the onion and fry for 10 minutes until softened and golden brown, then stir in the tomato, spices and salt and cook for a further 5 minutes. Stir in the curry leaves and green chillies and remove from the heat.

Preheat the oven to 200°C/gas 6. Heat the coconut or vegetable oil in a large frying pan over a high heat and fry the fish for 1–2 minutes on each side to brown slightly, but not to cook the fish through.

Cut out 4 pieces of foil large enough to wrap each fish. Place a spoonful of the masala in the centre of each, spreading it out a little. Place a fish on top then spread the remaining masala over each fish. Fold the foil into parcels and place on a baking tray. Cook in the oven for 12 minutes until the core temperature is 60°C. Unwrap the parcels at the table to serve.

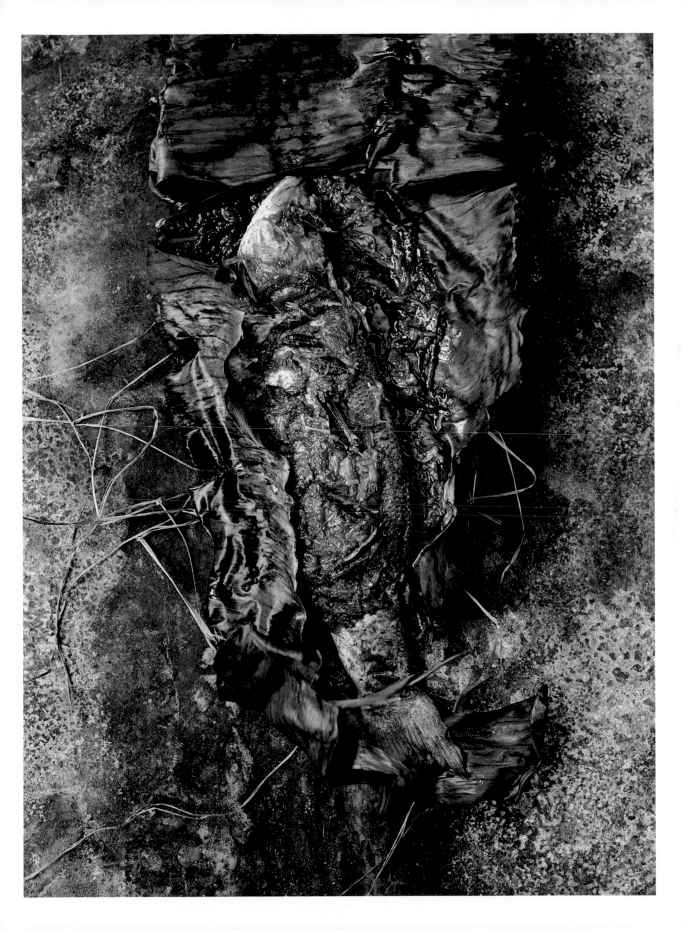

Poached gilthead bream with mousseline sauce and pilaf rice

Alternative fish:
bass, gurnard,
mussel cracker,
red mullet, snapper

SERVES 4
2 gilthead bream, each
    weighing 350–400g,
    scaled and gutted
    (see page 16)
Salt

For the mousseline sauce
50ml double cream
225g butter
2 egg yolks
¾ tsp salt
2 tbsp water
juice of ½ lemon

For the rice
1 small shallot,
    finely chopped
5g butter
1 fresh bay leaf
150g short-grain
    paella rice
½ tsp salt
180ml water

Few people appreciate the pleasure of warm poached fish, aside from salmon. Though this recipe is simple, the aim is to show how to poach a fish perfectly and how to fillet the cooked fish for your guests.

A fish kettle is the ideal pan for cooking whole fish (see page 48), but if you don't have one, use a pan big enough to take the fish lying flat. Barely cover the fish with water and season with salt at the ratio of 1 teaspoon of salt per 600ml of water. Bring the water to the boil, simmer for 6 minutes, then check the core temperature of the fish using a probe. When the temperature reaches 60°C, lift the fish carefully out of the water and lay on its side on a chopping board. Scrape away the fins with a knife, then cut through the skin just behind the head and at the tail, and peel the skin away. Cut the fish along the backbone and push the two upper fillets away, laying them neatly on the chopping board. Lift the head and backbone away from the two lower fillets. Turn the bottom half over on the chopping board and curl away the skin. Place these two fillets skinned-side down on a serving plate and lay the other two fillets on top. Do the same with the other fish and keep warm.

To make the sauce, whip the cream till it starts to form ribbons. Melt the butter in a small pan, bring to the boil, then turn down the heat and drain off the clarified butter, leaving the solids behind. Put the egg yolks, salt, water and lemon juice in a blender, then pour in the clarified butter in a steady stream with the motor running. Remove the sauce to a bowl and fold in the whipped cream.

To prepare the rice, fry the shallots gently in the butter with the bay leaf in a small saucepan. Add the rice and salt, and stir. Pour on the water, bring to the boil, cover and turn the heat down to a very low simmer. Simmer for 10 minutes, then leave with the heat off for another 3 minutes. Serve the fish with the rice and the sauce separately.

Amritsari fish

Alternative fish:
bream, dab, flounder,
gurnard, latchet,
leatherjacket, megrim
sole, plaice, pouting,
silver perch, tilapia,
whiting

SERVES 3-6
3 x 150g fillets of sea
    bream, each cut into 2
2cm fresh ginger,
    finely grated
1 large garlic clove,
    finely crushed
2 tsp vegetable oil

For the batter
50g chickpea flour
1 tsp turmeric powder
½ tsp salt
1 egg, lightly beaten
1cm fresh ginger,
    finely grated
1 small garlic clove,
    finely crushed
2–3 tbsp cold water
Vegetable oil, for deep frying

To serve
Chat masala (see page 312)
Lemon wedges
Kachumber salad
    (see page 315)

Indians treat their abundant river fish as they might mutton or paneer, and cook it with spicy accompaniments. Here I've given farmed bream the same treatment. The chickpea flour in the batter gives the fish a pleasing savouriness.

For the fish, mix together the ginger, garlic and vegetable oil, then rub this over the fillets and leave to marinate for 15 minutes.

To make the batter, sift the chickpea flour, turmeric and salt into a bowl. Mix the egg with the ginger, garlic and water. Whisk the liquid into the flour, adding a little more water if needed, until you have a smooth batter with the consistency of double cream.

Heat vegetable oil for deep-frying over a medium-high heat. Drop a tiny amount of batter into the hot oil to check it's hot enough; the batter should rise and bubble. Coat the fish in the batter, carefully add to the hot oil and fry for 2–3 minutes, turning once, until golden and crisp. Remove with a slotted spoon and drain on kitchen paper. Sprinkle with a pinch of chat masala and serve with lemon wedges and kachumber salad.

Chargrilled butterflied sea bream

*Alternative fish:
blue warehou, bream,
coral trout, garfish,
King George whiting,
sea bass, silver perch,
snapper, snoek, spangled
emperor, sweetlip*

SERVES 4

4 x 350g sea bream, gutted
   and scaled (see page 16)
25g shallots, roughly chopped
15g (3 cloves) garlic,
   roughly chopped
1 red bird's-eye chilli,
   thinly sliced
15g peeled fresh ginger,
   roughly chopped
7g peeled fresh galangal
   or extra ginger,
   roughly chopped
10g peeled fresh turmeric,
   roughly chopped, or
   ½ tsp turmeric powder
2 tbsp Tamarind water
   (see page 312)
½ tsp salt
4 tbsp vegetable oil
Sambal matah
   (see page 314), to serve

The Balinese cook has prepared the fish in the photograph by splitting it down the backbone from the head to the tail, gutting it and opening it flat joined at the belly. You could try this if you haven't got your fish ready gutted from the fishmonger. For a gutted fish, butterfly it as described in the recipe.

Trim the fins from the fish, then working with one fish at a time, open up the belly cavity down to the tail. Split the head almost in half by cutting from under the mouth up towards the top of the head but not quite all the way through. Open up and press firmly along the backbone until the fish is completely flat.

For the marinade, put the shallots, garlic, chilli, ginger, galangal, turmeric, tamarind water and salt into a mini food processor and blend to a smooth paste.

Tip into a small bowl and stir in 2 tablespoons of the oil. Paint some of the marinade over both sides of each fish and leave for at least 10 minutes. Stir the remaining vegetable oil into the remaining marinade. If you are not barbecuing, preheat the grill to hot.

If you have one, place the fish in a lightly oiled wire fish grill: this makes turning it easier. Otherwise, simply place the fish on the oiled bars of the barbecue or the rack of the grill pan, skin-side up. Cook for 4 minutes on each side, basting regularly with the leftover marinade, until slightly charred and cooked through. Serve straight away with the sambal matah.

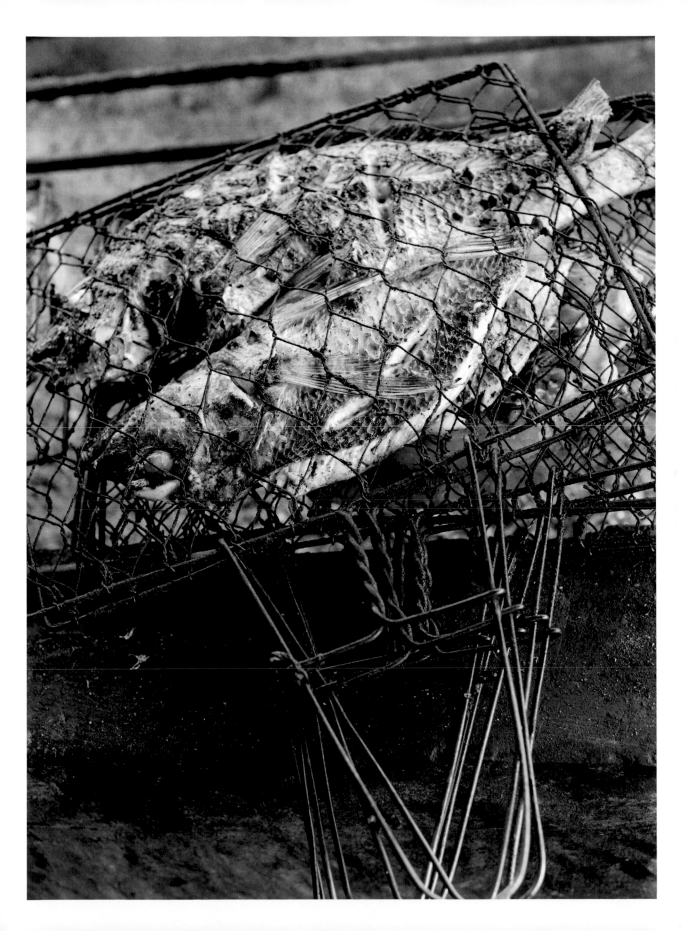

Madras fish curry of snapper, tomato and tamarind

Alternative fish:
blue-eye trevalla, hapuka,
gurnard, John Dory,
kinglip, mahi mahi,
monkfish, morwong,
sea bass, toothfish

SERVES 4–6
60ml vegetable oil
1 tbsp yellow mustard seeds
1 large onion, finely chopped
3 garlic cloves, finely crushed
30 fresh curry leaves
2 tsp Kashmiri chilli powder
2 tsp ground coriander
2 tsp turmeric powder
400g can chopped tomatoes
100ml Tamarind water
  (see page 312)
2 green chillies, each sliced
  lengthways into 6 pieces,
  with seeds
1 tsp salt
700g snapper fillets,
  cut into 5cm chunks

In my *India* book, I nominated this as my favourite curry. I can still remember the slightly oily flavour of the exquisite snapper because fish oil, when perfectly fresh, is very nice to eat. I always think oily fish goes well with curry anyway, particularly with the tomatoes, tamarind and curry leaves. Serve with plain rice.

Heat the oil in a heavy-based saucepan over a medium heat. When hot, add the mustard seeds and fry for 30 seconds, then stir in the onion and garlic and fry gently for about 10 minutes until softened and lightly golden.

Add the curry leaves, chilli powder, coriander and turmeric and fry for 2 minutes, then stir in the tomatoes, tamarind water, green chillies and salt and simmer for about 10 minutes until rich and reduced. Add the fish, cook for a further 5 minutes or until just cooked through, and serve.

Chargrilled snapper with a mango, prawn and chilli salsa

Alternative fish:
barramundi, bass,
blue-eye trevalla, bream,
dhufish, grey mullet,
gurnard, hapuka,
John Dory, monkfish,
mulloway, red mullet,
salmon, stumpnose

SERVES 4
4 x 175g snapper fillets
Extra virgin olive oil
Salt and freshly ground
   black pepper
Coriander sprigs,
   to garnish

For the salsa
2 large medium-hot red chillies
100g peeled cooked tiger
   prawns, thickly sliced
4 spring onions, thinly sliced
1 small garlic clove,
   finely chopped
1 ripe but firm avocado, diced
½ ripe but firm mango, diced
Juice of 1 lime
A pinch of salt

An almost ripe mango with plenty of acidity will combine well with the avocado, chilli and spring onions for a powerful flavour combination.

For the salsa, cut the chillies in half lengthways and scrape out the seeds with the tip of a small knife but leave the ribs behind to give the salsa some heat, then cut across into thin slices. Mix all the ingredients together.

Brush the snapper fillets on both sides with olive oil and season well with salt and pepper. Cut each one into 3, slightly on the diagonal.

Cook the pieces of snapper either skin-side down on the griddle or barbecue, or skin-side up under the grill, for 3–4 minutes.

To serve, spoon the salsa on to 4 plates and place the strips of fish on top. Drizzle oil around the edge and garnish with coriander sprigs.

Monkfish vindaloo

Alternative fish:
Australian salmon (kahawai),
coley, haddock, hake, hapuka,
kingfish, mahi mahi, pollock,
salmon, snoek, Spanish
mackerel, swordfish, yellowtail

SERVES 4
60ml vegetable oil
1 medium onion, chopped
2 tomatoes, roughly chopped
300ml water
1 tsp salt
4 medium-hot green chillies,
   cut lengthways in half
900g skinned monkfish tail,
   sliced across into steaks
   2.5cm thick (see page 25)
Coconut vinegar or white
   wine vinegar, to taste
Rick's everyday pilau rice
   (see page 314), to serve

For the vindaloo curry paste
40g dried Kashmiri chillies
1 tsp black peppercorns
1½ tsp cloves
7cm cinnamon stick
1 tsp cumin seeds
1 tsp turmeric powder
1 small onion, chopped
40g fresh ginger
40g (about 8 cloves)
   garlic, peeled
50g tamarind paste
1 tsp sugar
2 tbsp coconut vinegar
   or white wine vinegar

This is the recipe I brought back from Goa after my first visit in the late 1980s. It uses lots of Kashmiri chillies, which are of medium heat. Use fewer chillies if cooking with hotter ones. The finished curry sauce should be quite thick and well reduced.

For the vindaloo paste, soak the chillies for 20 minutes. Put the peppercorns, cloves, cinnamon and cumin seeds into a mortar or spice grinder and grind to a fine powder. Tip the powder into a mini food processor and add the drained chillies, the turmeric, onion, ginger, garlic, tamarind, sugar and vinegar. Blend to a smooth paste.

Heat the oil in a large, deep frying pan. Add the onion and fry over a moderate heat for 10 minutes. Stir in the vindaloo paste and fry gently for 5 minutes. Add the tomatoes, water and salt, and leave the sauce to simmer for 20 minutes, giving it a stir every now and then.

Add the green chillies with the monkfish and simmer for 10 minutes, turning the fish once. Add more vinegar and salt to taste, and serve with the pilau rice.

Ceviche of monkfish with avocado

*Alternative fish:
flathead, flounder,
gurnard, hapuka,
John Dory, kinglip,
mahi mahi, trigger fish*

SERVES 6
500g monkfish fillets,
   sliced (see page 25)
Juice of 3 limes and 1 orange
1 medium-hot red chilli,
   halved and thinly sliced
1 small red onion, halved
   and thinly sliced
6 tomatoes, skinned
   and chopped
3 tbsp extra virgin olive oil
2 tbsp roughly chopped
   coriander
1 tsp salt
1 large ripe but firm avocado

The citrus juice 'cooks' the fish, and I am in favour of minimizing the 'cooking' so that the result is somewhere between ceviche and sashimi.

Put the monkfish pieces into a shallow dish. Pour over the citrus juice. Cover and refrigerate for 10 minutes, during which time the fish will turn white and opaque.

Lift the monkfish out of the juice with a slotted spoon and put into a large bowl with the chilli, onion, tomato, olive oil, coriander and salt. Toss together lightly.

Halve the avocado, remove the stone and peel. Chop into dice. Pile the ceviche on to plates with the avocado and serve at once.

Pan-fried fillet of monkfish with new season's garlic and fennel

Alternative fish: barramundi, blue cod, blue-eye trevalla, cod, coley, flathead, grouper, gurnard, haddock, hake, John Dory, marlin, murray cod, swordfish, toothfish

SERVES 4

16 large garlic cloves, ideally new season
100g semolina
15g sprigs of fennel herb
100g unsalted butter
500g fennel bulb, thinly sliced
600ml Fish stock (see page 310)
Salt and freshly ground black pepper
4 x 200g pieces of prepared monkfish fillet (see page 25)
4 tbsp sunflower oil
2 tsp lemon juice
A splash of Pernod or Ricard

The very tender-skinned fresh garlic that arrives in the UK in May and June is perfect for this dish and you don't even have to peel it. But this recipe is good made with any garlic. Stirring in a few sliced leaves of ransomes – wild garlic – at the same time as the fennel herb would give the dish a garlicky lift too. If using thinner fillets of one of the alternative fish, simple pan-frying will be enough; no need to fire up the oven.

Put 2 garlic cloves, the semolina and all but 1 sprig of fennel into a food processor. Blend to an aromatic pale green powder.

Cut the rest of the garlic cloves lengthways into long thin pieces. Melt half the butter in a pan, add the garlic and sliced fennel and fry over a medium heat until lightly browned. Add the fish stock and seasoning and simmer for 15 minutes until the fennel is tender.

Preheat the oven to 200°C/gas 6. Coat the monkfish in the semolina mixture. Heat the oil in an ovenproof frying pan, add a small knob of butter and the monkfish pieces and fry over a moderate heat, turning now and then, until golden brown all over. Transfer the pan to the oven and cook the monkfish for a further 10 minutes.

Take the monkfish from the oven and slice diagonally into thick pieces; keep warm. Add the sautéed fennel mixture, lemon juice, Pernod and remaining fennel herb, finely chopped, to the pan in which the monkfish was cooked. Simmer rapidly until slightly reduced, then add the remaining butter and simmer until it has blended in to make a rich sauce. Serve the fish with sauce spooned around it.

Rice with monkfish, saffron and red peppers

Alternative fish: barramundi, bass, blue cod, bream, grey mullet, gurnard, John Dory, latchet, mahi mahi, red mullet, snapper, tarakihi

SERVES 6

4 tbsp olive oil
75g finely chopped shallot
1 small head of garlic, cloves finely chopped
Pimentón dulce (smoked sweet Spanish paprika)
A pinch of crushed dried chillies
200g tomatoes, chopped
1 litre Fish stock (see page 310)
½ tsp loosely packed saffron strands
1½ tsp salt, plus extra for seasoning
400g short-grain paella rice, such as Calasparra
1 large Roasted red pepper (see page 312) or 3 pimientos from a jar
500g monkfish fillet, trimmed of all membrane then cut across into 1cm-thick slices (see page 25)
1 quantity Aïoli (see page 311), to serve

There are many 'dry' rice dishes (arroces secos) in the Valencia region of Spain other than the paella we all know – and this is a very good one.

Heat 2 tablespoons of the olive oil in a shallow flameproof casserole, add the shallot and fry gently for 10 minutes or until soft and sweet but not browned. Add the garlic, ½ teaspoon of pimentón and the chillies and fry for 2 more minutes, then stir in the tomatoes and cook until they have broken down into a sauce. Stir in the fish stock, saffron and salt and bring to the boil, stirring. Sprinkle in the rice, stir once, then leave to simmer vigorously over a medium-high heat for 6 minutes.

Cut the roasted red pepper or pimientos into 1cm-wide strips, discarding any skin or seeds. Sprinkle them over the top of the rice and shake the pan so they sink into the mixture a little. Lower the heat and leave to simmer gently for another 12 minutes. At the end of this time almost all the liquid should be absorbed and the rice will be pitted with small holes.

Pat the monkfish pieces dry on kitchen paper and season with salt and a little pimentón. Heat the remaining 2 tablespoons of oil in a non-stick frying pan. Add the monkfish slices a few at a time and fry over a high heat for 1 minute on each side until very lightly coloured and almost cooked through.

Lay the fish on top of the rice, turn off the heat and cover the casserole with a tea towel, opened-out newspaper or lid. Leave to rest for 5 minutes, during which time the monkfish will finish cooking through. Serve warm with the aïoli.

Tandoori fish with naans

Alternative fish:
Arctic char, Australian salmon (kahawai), bonito, conger eel, dogfish, grey mullet, John Dory, ling, marlin, morwong, ocean trout, Pacific halibut, salmon, sea trout, Spanish mackerel, swordfish, tuna

SERVES 4

For the fish
Juice of ½ lemon
1 tsp Kashmiri chilli powder
1 tsp turmeric powder
½ tsp salt
500g monkfish fillet, cut into
   5cm chunks (see page 25)

For the tandoori paste
1 tsp fennel seeds
1 tsp caraway seeds
½ tsp Kashmiri chilli powder
½ tsp salt
50g natural yogurt
30g cashew nuts
3cm fresh ginger,
   roughly chopped
2 garlic cloves,
   roughly chopped
1 tsp beetroot powder
   (for colour; optional)

To serve
Pinch of Chat masala
   (see page 312)
Garlic butter naans
   (see page 315)

Any food from the tandoor oven cries out to be accompanied by my favourite bread in India, also from the tandoor: naan. To make your own, see page 315.

Preheat the oven to its highest setting. Mix together the lemon juice, chilli powder, turmeric and salt. Rub all over the fish pieces and set aside for 5 minutes.

For the tandoori paste, put the fennel seeds, caraway seeds, chilli powder and salt into a spice grinder and blend to a powder. Transfer the ground spices to a mini food processor with the yogurt, cashew nuts, ginger, garlic and beetroot powder, if using, and blend to a paste.

Rub the paste all over the marinated fish, then arrange the fish on a wire rack over a roasting tin and place on the top shelf of the oven. Cook for 5 minutes, or until just cooked through. Sprinkle with chat masala and serve with naans.

Confit of salmon with a salad of sweet dill pickled vegetables and crisp lettuce

See technique on page 50.

SERVES 4 AS A
FIRST COURSE
4 x 100g fillets salmon
50g daikon (mooli) or other
  radish, peeled and cut into
  thin strips (julienne)
50g red onion, thinly sliced
50g cucumber, preferably
  a small one, thinly sliced
8 cos or baby gem
  lettuce leaves
Extra virgin olive oil
Salt
50g Mustard mayonnaise
  (see page 311) or Japanese
  Kewpie or Hellmann's
30ml water
30g apple, cut into thin
  strips (julienne)

For the pickling liquid
100ml white wine vinegar
40g white sugar
1 tsp salt
50ml water
2cm red chilli, thinly sliced
Small handful of dill, chopped

The salmon fillets are cooked in a plastic bag in a bath of water at 50°C until the core temperature of the fillet is just 40°C. The fish is then beautifully soft but not raw. The lettuce leaves in the salad can be scorched with a blowtorch to give the salad a pleasing charred flavour. The recipe is a collaboration between me and Jack, my son, showing the old dog a few tricks.

Make the confit of salmon as shown on page 50. To make the pickle, mix all the ingredients except a teaspoon of the dill, which you will add to the mayonnaise sauce.

Put the radish, red onion and cucumber in a bowl with the pickling liquid for 5 minutes, then strain off. Keep the rest of the liquid in the fridge for other dishes.

Brush the lettuce leaves with a little olive oil and season with a sprinkle of salt. If you have a blowtorch, scorch the leaves, creating a few brown spots.

Warm the mayonnaise with the water in a small pan; don't boil it.

To serve, place each confit of salmon on a warmed plate, with a neat pile of vegetables and apple, and the scorched lettuce leaves. Drizzle the mayonnaise around, sprinkle with chopped dill and add the warm salmon.

Gravlax (dill-cured salmon)

See technique on page 66.

Alternative fish:
ocean trout, sea trout

SERVES 6

2 x 750g skin-on
   salmon fillets
1 large bunch dill,
   roughly chopped
100g coarse sea salt
75g white sugar
2 tbsp crushed white
   peppercorns

For the horseradish
and mustard sauce
2 tsp finely grated horseradish
   (fresh or from a jar)
2 tsp finely grated onion
1 tsp Dijon mustard
1 tsp caster sugar
2 tbsp white wine vinegar
A good pinch of salt
175ml double cream

Making your own gravlax is absolutely worthwhile. You never get quite the same intense dill flavour if you buy it. I particularly like the flavour of the white peppercorns in this cure.

Put one of the salmon fillets, skin-side down, on to a large sheet of cling film. Mix the dill with the salt, sugar and crushed peppercorns and spread it over the salmon. Place the other fillet on top, skin-side up.

Tightly wrap in 2 or 3 layers of cling film and lift on to a large, shallow tray. Rest a slightly smaller tray or chopping board on top of the fish and weigh it down. Refrigerate for 2 days, turning the fish every 12 hours so that the briny mixture, which has developed inside the parcel, bastes the outside of the fish.

For the horseradish and mustard sauce, stir together all the ingredients except for the cream. Whip the cream into soft peaks, stir in the horseradish mixture, cover and chill.

Remove the fish from the briny mixture and slice it as you would smoked salmon, then serve with the sauce.

Whole salmon baked in foil with tarragon

See technique on page 49.

Alternative fish:
Arctic char, blue fish,
kingfish, ocean trout,
salmon trout, trout,
yellowtail

SERVES 4

50g butter, melted
1 x 1.5kg salmon, cleaned
    and trimmed (see page 16)
1 small bunch tarragon,
    roughly chopped
120ml dry white wine
Juice of ½ lemon
Salt and freshly ground
    black pepper
1 quantity Beurre blanc
    (see page 311), to serve

Tarragon has a great affinity with salmon, and here I've used plenty. Boiled new potatoes go very well with this.

Preheat the oven to 220°C/gas 7. Brush the centre of a large sheet of foil with some of the melted butter. Place the salmon in the centre and bring the edges of the foil up around the fish slightly. Put the open parcel on to a large baking sheet.

Mix the tarragon with the rest of the melted butter, plus the wine, lemon juice, salt and pepper. Spoon the mixture into the cavity of the fish and over the top. Bring the sides of the foil up over the fish and pinch together, folding over the edges a few times to make a loose airtight parcel. Bake for 20–25 minutes. Ideally, use a thermometer and take it out of the oven when the core temperature reaches 55°C.

Remove the fish from the oven and open up the parcel. If you wish, remove the skin as follows: cut through the skin just behind the head and above the tail and lift it off. Carefully turn the fish over and repeat on the other side. Lift the salmon on to a warmed serving dish and serve with the beurre blanc.

Salmon en croûte with currants and ginger

See technique on page 57.

Alternative fish:
Arctic char, blue fish,
kingfish, ocean trout,
salmon trout, yellowtail

SERVES 6

2 x 550g pieces of skinned
   salmon fillet, taken from
   behind the gut cavity of
   a 3–4kg fish (see page 46,
   steps 1 and 2)
Salt
100g unsalted butter, softened
4 pieces of stem ginger in
   syrup, well drained and
   finely diced
25g currants
½ tsp ground mace
Freshly ground black pepper
750g chilled puff pastry
1 egg, beaten, to glaze

No fish cookery book would be complete without a recipe for salmon cooked in puff pastry. It's a rich and filling dish, and you don't need a lot per person.

Season the salmon fillets well on both sides with salt. Mix the softened butter with the stem ginger, currants, mace, ½ teaspoon of salt and some black pepper. Spread the inner face of 1 salmon fillet evenly with the butter mixture and then lay the second fillet on top.

Roll out the pastry and create the salmon parcel as shown on page 57. Chill the salmon en croûte for at least an hour.

Preheat the oven to 200°C/gas 6 and put in a large baking sheet to heat up. Remove the salmon en croûte from the fridge and brush all over with beaten egg.

Take the hot baking sheet out of the oven and carefully transfer the salmon parcel on to it. Return it to the oven and bake for 35–40 minutes, or until the core temperature reaches 55°C using a thermometer.

Remove the salmon en croûte and leave to rest for 5 minutes. Transfer it to a warmed serving plate and take it to the table whole. Cut it across into slices to serve.

Grilled miso salmon with rice noodles, spring onions and beansprouts

Alternative fish: kingfish, tuna

SERVES 4

4 x 150g salmon steaks
50ml vegetable oil
15g (3 cloves) garlic, grated
20g fresh ginger, grated
8 spring onions, sliced
1 medium red chilli, thinly sliced
200g dried rice noodles, boiled for 3 minutes and drained
100g beansprouts
A small handful of coriander, chopped
1 tbsp fish sauce

For the miso glaze
10g red miso paste
2 tsp balsamic vinegar
2 tsp soy sauce
1 tsp hot smoked paprika, Spanish pimentón
1 tbsp water

This is designed for steaks of large oily fish. It's best if the fish is grilled medium rare: to about 50°C in the centre, measured using a temperature probe.

Mix together the ingredients for the miso glaze and use to paint the fish steaks. Place the steaks on an oiled grilling tray. Turn on the grill.

Heat the oil in a wok and stir-fry the garlic, ginger, spring onions and chilli for a couple of minutes, then add the noodles, beansprouts and coriander.

Grill the fish steaks for about 5 minutes, turning once. Stir the fish sauce into the stir-fried vegetables, then arrange on plates and top with the fish to serve.

Pan-fried trout with crisp ham

Alternative fish:
Arctic char, sea trout

SERVES 2
4 tbsp olive oil
6 small, thin slices of
    air-dried ham, such
    as Spanish serrano
2 x 300–350g rainbow
    trout, cleaned
Salt and freshly ground
    black pepper
50g plain flour,
    for coating
1 fat garlic clove,
    finely chopped
25g butter
Juice of ½ lemon
A small handful of
    flat-leaf parsley
    leaves, chopped

Here, the trout is pan-fried then transferred to the oven for a perfectly golden crust. I recommend using a thermal probe: the fish will be moist and ready when the temperature at the centre reaches 58°C.

Preheat the oven to 200°C/gas 6. Heat the oil in a heavy-based frying pan over a medium heat. Add 4 of the slices of ham and fry for a few seconds on each side until the fat has rendered out and flavoured the oil, and the ham is crisp and lightly golden. Remove to a plate. Finely chop the remaining 2 ham slices and set aside.

Season the belly cavity of each fish with a little salt, then place 2 slices of the crisp ham inside each one. Season the outside of the fish, then dust them in the flour, knocking off the excess.

Return the pan to a medium heat and add the fish. Fry for 2 minutes on each side until golden brown, then carefully transfer to a lightly oiled baking dish and bake for 5 minutes. Set the frying pan to one side.

Remove the trout from the oven, cover loosely with foil and leave somewhere warm to cook on for a further 3–4 minutes. Return the frying pan to the heat, add the chopped ham and fry briefly over a high heat until starting to become golden and crispy. Turn down the heat, add the garlic and butter to the pan and continue frying until the butter is nut-brown and the garlic is starting to colour. Add the lemon juice and parsley, spoon the mixture over the trout and serve.

Swordfish passanda with chilli, almonds, yogurt and cardamom

Alternative seafood:
John Dory, leatherjacket,
monkfish; cuttlefish,
prawns, squid, trigger fish

MAKES ABOUT
50 PIECES
3cm cinnamon stick
Seeds from 2 cardamom pods
1 tsp coriander seeds
3 tbsp vegetable oil
1 small onion, grated (100g)
15g garlic (3 cloves), grated
20g fresh ginger, grated
½ tsp turmeric powder
½ tsp chilli powder,
   such as Kashmiri
200g yogurt
200g tomatoes, chopped
2 tbsp ground almonds
1 tsp salt
½ tsp sugar
50ml water
500g swordfish fillet,
   cut into 2 x 2cm pieces

To serve
Coriander, chopped
Poppadoms (optional)

This take on a mild North Indian dish has been designed for serving at a drinks party, either on cocktail skewers or on quarters of mini poppadoms puffed up in the microwave. Swordfish works because the fish needs to be firm-textured, but do check out the list of alternative options too.

Grind the cinnamon, cardamom and coriander seeds in a spice grinder.

Heat the oil, add the onion, garlic and ginger, and cook gently for 10 minutes. Add the freshly ground spices, the turmeric and chilli, stir for 30 seconds, then add the yogurt, tomatoes, almonds, salt, sugar and water.

Simmer until reduced by three-quarters, then gently stir in the fish and cook for 3–4 minutes. The sauce should be coating the fish well. Sprinkle with coriander and serve with cocktail sticks or on pieces of poppadom.

Grilled sardines with coarsely chopped green herbs

Alternative fish: anchovies, small herring, horse mackerel (scad), small mackerel, smelts, sprats

SERVES 4 AS A
FIRST COURSE
1 tsp finely grated
  lemon zest
½ tbsp finely chopped
  rosemary
1 tbsp finely chopped
  parsley
1 garlic clove,
  very finely chopped
½ tbsp finely chopped
  pitted green olives
½ tbsp chopped capers
½ tsp sea salt flakes
¼ tsp freshly ground
  black pepper
8 sardines, cleaned and
  trimmed (see page 18)
Extra virgin olive oil, for
  brushing and serving
Lemon wedges, to serve

It's important to remember to soak bamboo skewers in cold water for at least half an hour before using so they don't scorch.

Mix together the lemon zest, rosemary, parsley, garlic, olives, capers, salt and pepper. Set to one side.

Preheat the grill to high. Pierce each sardine from head to tail with a skewer. Lay them on a lightly oiled baking tray and sprinkle them with some extra virgin olive oil, salt and pepper. Grill for 2 minutes on each side.

Serve the skewered sardines scattered with the herb mixture, drizzled with a little extra oil and with the lemon wedges alongside.

Split herrings with a caper and fresh tomato salsa

Alternative fish:
horse mackerel (scad),
mackerel, sand
whiting, sardines

SERVES 4
4 x 200g herrings,
   fins trimmed
   (see page 16, step 2)
Salt and freshly ground
   black pepper

For the salsa
200g vine-ripened
   tomatoes, roughly diced
1 garlic clove,
   very finely chopped
25g capers in brine,
   drained and rinsed
1 tbsp coarsely chopped
   flat-leaf parsley

All of the herring family – pilchards, sprats and herrings – when cooked perfectly fresh are among the best things you could ever eat. Ideal for barbecuing.

Preheat the grill to high. Remove the bones from the herrings as described on page 18. Sprinkle them with a little salt and pepper on both sides, then place them on a lightly oiled baking tray and grill for 2 minutes on each side.

For the salsa, mix together the tomatoes, garlic, capers, parsley and some seasoning. Serve the herrings with the salsa.

Pondicherry mackerel fish fry

Alternative fish:
Arctic char, herring,
kingfish, sand
whiting, shad, snoek,
Spanish mackerel

SERVES 4
125g natural yogurt
50g (10 cloves) garlic,
   finely crushed
2 tbsp Kashmiri
   chilli powder
1 tsp salt
Juice of ½ lime
50–100ml water
8 fresh mackerel fillets
   (see page 20)
3 tbsp vegetable oil
A handful of coriander
   leaves, chopped
A pinch of salt
Lime wedges, to serve

Now a firm favourite at Rick Stein's Fish in Falmouth. Add a little more marinade to the final frying, if you like, but don't get the oil too hot or it will flare up when you add the water-based marinade. This is just what you should do with fish: simple, but spicy.

Mix together the yogurt, garlic, chilli powder, salt and lime juice in a large bowl, then stir in enough water to give the consistency of double cream (the amount will depend on the brand of yogurt and the juiciness of the lime).

Add the mackerel fillets and turn them over to coat in the yogurt mixture.

Set aside to marinate for 5–10 minutes. Pat dry with kitchen paper.

Heat the oil in a large frying pan over a medium heat. When the oil is hot, fry the mackerel in batches for 3 minutes on each side. Finish with some more of the marinade.

Sprinkle with coriander leaves and salt, and serve with lime wedges.

Mackerel recheado

See technique on page 21.

Alternative fish: flathead, flounder, herring, plaice, pomfret, sardines, shad, tilapia, trout, whiting

SERVES 4
4 x 200g mackerel

For the Goan masala paste
1 tsp cumin seeds
1 tsp coriander seeds
1 tsp black peppercorns
½ tsp fennel seeds
½ tsp cloves
½ tsp turmeric powder
50g medium-hot red
   chillies, roughly chopped
½ tsp salt
3 garlic cloves, chopped
1 tsp light muscovado sugar
1½ tsp Tamarind water
   (see page 312)
3cm fresh root ginger,
   roughly chopped
1 tablespoon red wine vinegar

The perfect accompaniments to mackerel recheado (or simply 'stuffed mackerel' in Portuguese) are Rick's everyday pilau rice (see page 314) and kachumber salad (see page 315).

Grind the spices in a spice grinder. Put them into a food processor with the rest of the ingredients and blend to a smooth paste.

Prepare the mackerel as described on page 21. Spread the cut face of one fillet with a teaspoon of the masala paste. Put the fish back into shape and tie in two places with string.

Barbecue or grill for 3 minutes on each side until crisp and lightly golden. Serve with pilau rice and kachumber salad.

Spicy green mango salad with smoked mackerel and a sweet and sour dressing

*Alternative fish:
any smoked oily fish
such as herring or
hot-smoked salmon*

SERVES 2

4 smoked mackerel
  fillets, weighing about
  275g in total
Vegetable oil, for deep-frying
1 green mango, about 500g
1 large carrot, about 75g
30g shallots, very
  thinly sliced
1 red bird's-eye chilli,
  finely chopped
25g roasted peanuts,
  roughly chopped
2 tsp palm sugar
1 tbsp fish sauce
About 1 tbsp lime juice,
  depending on the
  tartness of the mango
15g Thai sweet basil,
  roughly chopped

Still popular at the Seafood Restaurant, this salad is hot with bird's-eye chilli, but it needs to be for the correct balance of flavour. If you can't get green mango, kohlrabi works well.

Skin the smoked mackerel fillets and break the meat into small flakes. Pour 2cm oil into a pan and heat to 190°C. Sprinkle the fish into the oil and fry for 1 minute until crispy. It will all stick together at this point but don't worry. Lift out on to a tray lined with lots of kitchen paper and leave to cool, then break up into small pieces again.

Peel the green mango and carrot and shred into thin strips 3–4mm wide. Put the mango, carrot, shallots, chilli, peanuts and fried fish pieces into a large bowl and toss together. Mix the sugar with the fish sauce and lime juice, add to the salad with the basil and toss together again. Serve straight away.

Salad of griddled garfish with sun-dried tomatoes and fennel seeds

See technique on page 24.

*Alternative fish:
albacore tuna, small
blue fish (tailor),
horse mackerel (scad),
mackerel, red mullet,
sand whiting, sable fish
(black cod), trout*

SERVES 4

4 small garfish
3 tbsp olive oil
2 tsp lemon juice
1 tsp chopped thyme
1 tsp fennel seeds,
   lightly crushed
A pinch of dried chilli flakes
Sea salt and freshly ground
   black pepper
25g rocket
25g prepared curly endive
15g flat-leaf parsley leaves
15g chervil sprigs
4–6 sun-dried tomatoes
   in olive oil, drained
   and thinly sliced
1 tbsp sherry vinegar

The flavours both of fennel and chervil complement many fish dishes. If you can't get chervil, leave it out, or use about half as much tarragon instead.

Fillet the garfish as shown on page 24. Mix together the olive oil, lemon juice, thyme, fennel seeds, chilli flakes, ½ teaspoon of salt and some black pepper. Brush a little of this mixture over both sides of the fish and set aside for 5 minutes.

Toss the rocket, curly endive, parsley and chervil together and set aside.

Heat a cast-iron griddle until really hot. Reduce the heat slightly, add the garfish, skin-side down, and cook for 1–1½ minutes, turning them over halfway through. Transfer them to a plate to stop them from cooking further.

Arrange the fish, strips of sun-dried tomato and salad leaves on 4 plates. Add the remaining marinade and the sherry vinegar to the pan and swirl it around briefly. Spoon over the salad and around the edge of the plate, and serve.

Chargrilled tuna with salsa verde

Alternative fish:
Arctic char, ocean trout,
sable fish (black cod),
salmon, sea trout

SERVES 4
4 x 200g thick tuna
    loin steaks
Olive oil
Salt and freshly ground
    black pepper

For the salsa verde
3 tbsp flat-leaf
    parsley leaves
1 tbsp mint leaves
3 tbsp capers, drained
6 anchovy fillets
    in oil, drained
1 garlic clove
1 tsp Dijon mustard
Juice of ½ lemon
125ml extra virgin
    olive oil
½ tsp salt

Tuna has an open texture and so heat penetrates fast and it cooks quickly. The steaks in this recipe need just one minute on each side if your cast-iron griddle or barbecue is at the correct temperature. A dish of classic simplicity. There are worries about tuna stocks, but not in every part of the world; in Cornwall in the summer there is an abundance of albacore, which is excellent in this dish.

Chop the parsley, mint, capers, anchovy fillets and garlic together by hand on a board (if you prefer to chop them in a food processor, don't run it for long as you want the sauce to have plenty of rugged texture). Scoop them into a bowl and stir in the mustard, lemon juice, olive oil and salt.

Brush the tuna steaks on both sides with oil and season well. Place the cast-iron griddle over a high heat and leave it to get smoking hot, then drizzle it with a little oil. Cook the tuna steaks for 1 minute on each side until nicely striped from the griddle but still pink and juicy in the centre. Serve at once with salsa verde spooned on top.

Marinated tuna with passion fruit, lime and coriander

Alternative fish:
albacore tuna, bonito,
hiramasa kingfish,
ocean trout, salmon,
sea trout, yellowtail

SERVES 4

3cm-thick piece of tuna
  loin fillet, weighing
  about 400g
2 passion fruit, each
  weighing about 35g
1 tbsp lime juice
3 tbsp sunflower oil
1 medium-hot green
  chilli, finely chopped
1 tsp caster sugar
1½ tbsp finely chopped
  coriander
½ tsp salt and freshly
  ground black pepper

I came up with this one New Year's Eve in Sydney. It seemed to encapsulate everything I love about al fresco food in Australia – very good with salmon too.

Slice the fish across the grain into very thin slices. Lay the slices over the base of 4 large plates. Cover each one with cling film and set aside in the fridge for at least 1 hour, or until you are ready to serve.

To make the dressing, cut the passion fruit in half and scoop the pulp into a sieve set over a bowl. Rub the pulp through the sieve to extract the juice; discard the seeds. Stir in the lime juice, sunflower oil, green chilli, sugar, coriander, salt and pepper. To serve, uncover the plates, spoon over the dressing and spread it over the surface of the fish with the back of the spoon. Leave for 10 minutes before serving.

Ragout of sautéed turbot with serrano ham, spring vegetables and pea shoots

Alternative fish:
John Dory, gurnard,
flathead, monkfish

SERVES 4 AS A
FIRST COURSE
40g fresh or frozen peas
60g courgettes, thinly sliced
100g small asparagus,
    cut on the diagonal
    into 1cm pieces
250g turbot fillet, skinned,
    cut into 6–7cm pieces
1 tbsp vegetable oil
40g unsalted butter
40g serrano ham,
    cut into strips
10g preserved lemon,
    finely chopped
200ml Chicken stock
    (see page 310)
1 tsp white miso paste
30g pea shoots
Salt

As I say at the back of the book, turbot is possibly the best-tasting fish in the world. Don't think that this has to be made with expensive turbot, however. You can use any firm-textured fish.

Blanch the vegetables in boiling salted water as follows: peas 30 seconds; courgettes 30 seconds; asparagus 60 seconds.

Season the turbot pieces with a little salt and fry over a moderate heat using the vegetable oil and ½ teaspoon of the butter.

Put the ham, preserved lemon, chicken stock and miso paste into a small pan. Bring to the boil, add the rest of the butter and boil rapidly for a minute to emulsify the butter and reduce the volume a little. Stir in the vegetables and pea shoots, warm through and pour into 4 warmed soup plates. Top with the turbot pieces.

Braised fillet of turbot with slivers of potato, mushrooms and minced truffle

Alternative fish: barramundi, bass, blue cod, blue-eye trevalla, brill, John Dory, kinglip, murray cod, Pacific halibut, sole

SERVES 4

600ml Chicken stock
   (see page 310)
175g waxy main-crop potatoes
100g unsalted butter
1 thin slice of cooked ham,
   about 25g, finely diced
25g shallots, finely chopped
90ml dry vermouth,
   such as Noilly Prat
100g button mushrooms,
   thinly sliced
2 tsp lemon juice
1 tbsp minced truffle
Salt and freshly ground
   black pepper
750g piece of skin-on turbot
   fillet, cut into 8 pieces
   (see page 34)
1 tbsp chopped parsley

Though we use fresh truffles in season at the Seafood Restaurant, we also put this on the menu using minced truffle; you can buy small jars of it quite easily now. Do consider the alternative fish for this. Turbot is fiendishly expensive, and this is very much a restaurant dish, where customers must have turbot.

Put the chicken stock into a wide pan and boil rapidly until reduced by half.

Peel the potatoes and slice as thinly as you can, then cut them across into thin matchsticks.

Melt half the butter in a frying pan that is large enough to hold all the pieces of fish in one layer. Add the potatoes, ham and shallots and cook gently for 4–5 minutes.

Add the vermouth and chicken stock and simmer for about 8 minutes, until the potatoes are almost cooked. You can prepare the dish to this stage a few hours in advance.

Stir the mushrooms, lemon juice, minced truffle and some salt and pepper into the pan and then rest the pieces of turbot on top, skin-side down. Cover and simmer for about 6 minutes or until the fish is cooked through.

Remove the fish and keep warm. Add the remaining butter to the pan and boil rapidly for 10 minutes or until the sauce has thickened and the potatoes are just beginning to break up. Stir the parsley into the sauce, return the fish and serve.

Roasted tronçons of turbot with sauce vierge

Alternative fish:
blue cod, brill, large flounder,
hapuka, New Zealand turbot,
Pacific halibut, large plaice

SERVES 4

90ml extra virgin olive oil,
   plus extra for brushing
1 tsp chopped rosemary
1 tsp chopped thyme
1 bay leaf, very finely chopped
½ tsp crushed fennel seeds
1 tsp coarsely crushed
   black peppercorns
1 tsp sea salt flakes
4 x 200g tronçons of turbot
   (see page 34)

For the sauce vierge
90ml extra virgin olive oil
2 tbsp lemon juice
1 plum tomato,
   seeded and diced
8 black olives, pitted
   and cut into fine strips
2 small anchovy fillets in
   oil, drained and diced
1 garlic clove, finely chopped
1 heaped tsp coarsely
   chopped parsley
Salt and coarsely ground
   black pepper

Sauce vierge has the sort of understated appeal that suits turbot very well. Turbot is such a perfect fish it hardly needs any accompaniment at all.

Preheat the oven to 230°C/gas 8. Mix together the olive oil, chopped herbs, fennel seeds, peppercorns and sea salt in a small roasting tin. Add the pieces of turbot and turn them over so they are well coated.

For the sauce, put everything except the chopped parsley and seasoning into a small pan, ready to warm through just before serving.

Heat a heavy-based ovenproof frying pan over a high heat until smoking hot. Add the tronçons of turbot, dark-side down, to the pan and sear for about 1 minute until the skin has taken on a good colour. Turn them over, transfer the pan to the oven and roast for 8–10 minutes. Just as the fish is ready, place the sauce over a very low heat to warm through.

Stir the parsley and seasoning into the sauce and serve it spooned around the fish. Brush the top of each piece of fish with a little oil and sprinkle with a few sea salt flakes.

A casserole of dab with spring onions, red wine and wild mushrooms

SERVES 2

400ml Chicken stock
 (see page 310)
15g dried porcini
60g unsalted butter
50g wild mushrooms,
 cleaned and sliced
Salt
12 spring onions,
 white part only (5cm)
4 garlic cloves, peeled
60g smoked back bacon,
 cut into thin strips
1 tsp balsamic vinegar
50ml deep red wine
A pinch of chilli powder
Leaves from 1 sprig of thyme
300g skin-on dab fillets

I came up with this as a way to serve fish with red wine. Something like a Cabernet Franc from the Loire or a red Sancerre or Pinot Noir from Alsace would be perfect.

Reduce the stock by half by rapid boiling. Remove from the heat and soak the dried porcini in about 100ml of the stock until soft.

Melt 25g of the butter in a wide-based pan, add the wild mushrooms, season with salt and fry. Lift out and keep warm. Add the spring onions and garlic to the same pan and cook over a moderate heat until lightly browned. Add about 30ml of the stock and simmer gently with a lid on until the onions and garlic are tender, then add the soaked porcini and the soaking liquid, the smoked bacon, the balsamic vinegar, red wine, chilli and thyme.

Turn up the heat and boil rapidly until everything has reduced to a thick sticky glaze.

Heat a small knob of the remaining butter in a frying pan. Season the dab fillets with a little salt and fry them skin-side down, then transfer to the main pan skin-side up, add the rest of the stock and simmer with a lid on for 2–3 minutes to cook them. Transfer the fillets to a serving dish. Add the rest of the butter to the main pan and reduce the liquid again until the sauce will coat the back of a spoon. Add the fried mushrooms and pour it all around the fish.

Grilled scored plaice with roasted red pepper, garlic and oregano

See technique on page 31.

Alternative fish:
dab, flounder, plaice,
New Zealand turbot, sole

SERVES 4
4 x 500g plaice
1 Roasted red pepper
   (see page 312)
½ medium-hot red chilli,
   seeded and finely chopped
50ml extra virgin olive oil
1 large garlic clove,
   finely chopped
1 tsp chopped oregano
2 tsp lemon juice
1 tsp salt and some freshly
   ground black pepper

You will see on page 31 that the fish is 'close cut', in other words, all the side bones are removed. This makes it easier to eat.

Prepare the fish as shown on page 31. Remove the skin and seeds from the roasted red pepper and finely chop the flesh. Mix with the rest of the ingredients to make the marinade. Pour over the fish, making sure it goes right into the slashes.

Preheat the grill to high. Transfer the fish to baking trays, dark-side up. Depending on the size of your grill, cook them 1 or 2 at a time for 7–8 minutes or until the flesh is firm and white at the thickest part, just behind the head. Spoon over the remaining marinade 4 minutes before the end of cooking.

Also known just as 'Dover sole meunière', this is 'miller's style'. The dish gets its name from the light dusting of flour the fish is given before frying.

Dover sole à la meunière

See technique on page 36.

Alternative fish:
any flatfish

SERVES 2

2 x 400–450g Dover soles, trimmed and skinned (see page 36)

Salt and freshly ground white pepper

25g plain flour

4 tbsp vegetable oil

50g unsalted butter

2 tsp lemon juice

1 tbsp chopped parsley

1 lemon, cut into 6 wedges, to serve

Season the Dover soles with salt and white pepper. Dip on both sides into flour and then pat off the excess.

Heat the oil in a large well-seasoned or non-stick frying pan. Add one of the soles, lower the heat slightly and add a small piece of the butter. Fry over a moderate heat for 4–5 minutes, without moving, until richly golden.

Carefully turn the fish over and cook for a further 4–5 minutes until golden brown and cooked through. Lift on to a serving plate and keep warm. Repeat with the second fish. Remove the bones as described on page 36, steps 8–10.

Discard the frying oil and wipe the pan clean. Add the remaining butter and allow it to melt over a moderate heat. When the butter starts to smell nutty and turn light brown, add the lemon juice, parsley and some seasoning. Pour some of this beurre noisette over each fish and serve with the lemon wedges.

Roasted ray wings with chilli beans

Alternative fish:
any sustainable ray

SERVES 4
4 x 200g prepared ray
    wings (see page 38)
1 tsp paprika
1 tsp salt
1 tsp coarsely crushed
    black pepper
50g butter
3 tbsp sherry vinegar

For the chilli beans
350g dried cannellini
    beans, soaked in cold
    water overnight
2 tbsp extra virgin olive oil
1 garlic clove, finely chopped
2 medium-hot red chillies,
    finely chopped
1 small onion, finely chopped
350ml Chicken stock
    (see page 310)
2 beef tomatoes, diced
1 tsp chopped tarragon
Sea salt and freshly ground
    black pepper

I was thinking of dropping any reference to ray in this book because of worries about conservation, though there are plenty of rays in Australia, New Zealand and South Africa. Then I discovered that the Bristol Channel ray fishery is applying for Marine Stewardship Council accreditation, so by the time this book is published the situation might well have improved.

Drain the cannellini beans and put them into a pan with fresh water to cover. Bring to the boil, skimming off any froth as it rises to the surface. Cover and simmer for 1 hour until as tender as baked beans. Drain and set aside.

Preheat the oven to 200°C/gas 6. Sprinkle the ray wings on both sides with the paprika, salt and black pepper.

For the chilli beans, put the olive oil, garlic and red chillies in a pan over a medium heat. As soon as the garlic and chillies start to sizzle, add the onion and cook for 5 minutes until soft. Add the beans and 300ml of the stock and leave to simmer for 10 minutes.

To cook the ray wings, melt the butter in a roasting tin on the hob. Add the wings and lightly brown them for 1 minute on each side. Transfer to the oven and roast for 10 minutes.

Stir the tomatoes into the beans and simmer for a further 10 minutes. Stir in the tarragon and season with salt and pepper.

Place the ray wings on top of the beans. Put the roasting tin over a moderate heat, add the sherry vinegar and the rest of the chicken stock and leave it to boil for a minute or two, scraping up all the crusty bits from the bottom. Season, strain, then spoon over the top of the ray.

Pulpo a la feria

SERVES 4
1 octopus, about 750g
1 onion, peeled
4 bay leaves
Salt
½ tsp pimentón
    picante (smoked
    hot Spanish paprika)
50ml good olive oil
½–1 tsp sea salt flakes

Translated as 'Octopus, fairground style', this is the classic Galician way of serving it. Buy octopus with two rows of suckers on each tentacle, called the common octopus (*Octopus vulgaris*); it is noticeably more tender than any others.

Clean the octopus as described on page 94. Bring a large pan of water to the boil with the onion, bay leaves, and salt at the ratio of 1 teaspoon per 750ml. Add the octopus and simmer for at least 45 minutes. Test, then cook for a further 15–20 minutes if it is still a little tough.

Lift the octopus out of the pan and drain away all the excess water. Put it on a board, cut off the tentacles and slice each one on the diagonal into pieces about 5mm thick. Cut the body into similar-sized pieces. Sprinkle with the pimentón picante.

Warm the olive oil in a small pan and drizzle it over the octopus, then sprinkle with the sea salt and serve.

Cuttlefish with meatballs, prawns and peas

SERVES 6 AS A
FIRST COURSE
6 tbsp olive oil
2 garlic cloves, finely chopped
1 medium onion,
    finely chopped
90ml dry white wine
200g tomatoes, chopped
2 tsp tomato purée
15g slice crustless white bread
1½ tbsp milk
2 tbsp chopped flat-leaf parsley
200g minced chicken
250g minced pork
A little freshly grated nutmeg
Salt and freshly ground
    black pepper
375g cleaned cuttlefish
    (see page 96), cut into
    2cm-wide strips
6 large shell-on raw prawns
150ml Chicken stock
    (see page 310) or water
100g peas, fresh or frozen

For the picada
2 tbsp olive oil
2 fat garlic cloves,
    peeled but left whole
10g slice crustless white bread
10g toasted blanched almonds
1 tomato, skinned
    and chopped
1 tsp flat-leaf parsley leaves
1 tbsp cold water

Combining meat with seafood was traditionally a way of eking out an expensive ingredient – meat – with a cheap one: seafood. Nowadays the reverse is more true. Cuttlefish, however, is still good value for money, and goes well with the chicken and pork meatballs.

For the picada, heat the olive oil in a small frying pan over a medium heat. Add the garlic and bread and fry, turning now and then, until golden brown. Add to the bowl of a mini food processor with the almonds, tomato, parsley and water. Blend to a paste and set aside.

Put 2 tablespoons of the oil, half the garlic and the onion into a saucepan and fry for 10 minutes until soft, sweet and lightly golden. Add the wine, tomato and tomato purée and simmer, stirring occasionally, for 6–7 minutes until reduced and thickened.

For the meatballs, tear the bread into a small bowl, sprinkle with the milk and leave until soft. Add the remaining chopped garlic, the parsley, minced chicken and pork, nutmeg and ½ teaspoon each of salt and black pepper. Mix together well and shape into 3cm balls. Heat 2 tablespoons of oil in a large frying pan, add the meatballs and fry for 3 minutes, shaking the pan every now and then, until golden brown. Remove and set aside.

Heat the rest of the oil in the pan, add the cuttlefish and prawns and fry for 2 minutes. Set aside with the meatballs. Add the tomato sauce to the pan, stir in the picada and simmer for 2 minutes. Reduce the heat to medium, stir in the stock or water and bring to the boil. Add the peas, meatballs, prawns and cuttlefish and season to taste. Simmer for 5 minutes until any remaining liquid has reduced.

Hot and sour squid salad with chilli, lime leaf, mint and coriander

Alternative seafood: cuttlefish or small, tender octopus

SERVES 4-6
400g squid
1–2 small lettuces, such
    as little gem or romaine,
    broken into pieces
2 spring onions, halved
    and finely shredded
Small handful each of mint
    and coriander leaves

For the dressing
3 tbsp lime juice
3 tbsp fish sauce
1 red bird's-eye chilli,
    thinly sliced
1 tsp palm sugar
10g garlic, finely chopped
2 fat lemongrass stalks,
    outer layers removed
    and core finely chopped
1 kaffir lime leaf,
    finely shredded

I'm not in favour of boiling squid – in this recipe it is dropped into lightly salted boiling water and left for only 30 seconds so that it just cooks through.

Prepare the squid as shown on page 92.

Bring 1.5 litres of water and 2 teaspoons salt to the boil in a pan. Add the pieces of squid a small handful at a time and cook for 30 seconds until it has just turned white and opaque and curled up. Remove with a strainer, rinse briefly under cold water, tip into a colander and leave to drain well. Repeat with the remaining squid, bringing the water back to a gentle boil each time. When all the squid is cooked, leave it to cool to room temperature.

Combine the ingredients for the dressing. Scatter the lettuce leaves, shredded spring onions and herbs over a serving plate. Mix the dressing into the squid and spoon the squid over the salad, along with the excess dressing. Serve at once.

Stir-fried salt and pepper squid with red chilli and spring onion

Alternative seafood: cuttlefish

SERVES 4 AS A
FIRST COURSE
750g squid
½ tsp black peppercorns
½ tsp Sichuan peppercorns
1 tsp sea salt flakes
2 tbsp sunflower oil
1 medium-hot red
   chilli, thinly sliced
   on the diagonal
   (seeds removed,
   if you prefer)
3 spring onions,
   sliced on the diagonal

For the salad
¼ cucumber, peeled,
   halved and seeded
50g beansprouts
25g watercress,
   large stalks removed
2 tsp dark soy sauce
2 tsp roasted sesame oil
¼ tsp caster sugar
A pinch of salt

My version of salt and pepper squid differs from most in that it is just stir-fried, not deep-fried in flour or batter. I think this is much nicer so long as the squid is very fresh.

Prepare the squid as described on page 92.

For the salad, cut the cucumber lengthways into short strips. Toss with the beansprouts and watercress and set aside in the fridge until needed. Whisk together the soy sauce, sesame oil, sugar and salt.

Heat a small heavy-based frying pan over a high heat. Add the black and Sichuan peppercorns and dry-roast for a few seconds, shaking the pan now and then, until they darken slightly and become aromatic. Coarsely crush, then stir in the sea salt flakes.

Heat a wok over a high heat until smoking. Add half the oil and half the squid and stir-fry it for 2 minutes, until lightly coloured. Tip on to a plate, then repeat with the remaining oil and the rest of the squid. Return the first batch of squid to the wok and add 1 teaspoon of the salt and pepper mixture (the rest can be used in other stir-fries). Toss together for about 10 seconds, then add the red chilli and spring onions and toss together very briefly. Serve immediately, with the dressed salad alongside.

Mussel masala with coconut, ginger and green chillies

SERVES 2-4
1.5 kg mussels, cleaned
   (see page 86)
30ml coconut oil
1 tsp black mustard seeds
50g fresh or frozen coconut,
   grated or blitzed in a
   food processor
1 small onion, finely chopped
6cm fresh ginger, finely grated
4 garlic cloves, finely crushed
2 green chillies, seeds
   removed, thinly sliced
A handful of fresh curry leaves
1 tsp fennel seeds
1 tsp ground black pepper
1 tsp Garam masala
   (see page 314)
½ tsp Kashmiri chilli powder
½ tsp turmeric powder
1 tsp salt

This dish is based on a clam masala from the Keralan Backwaters of southern India, but I've used mussels instead as they're easier to get hold of.

Put a splash of water into a large saucepan, add the mussels, cover with a lid and cook over a high heat, shaking the pan every now and again until all the mussels have opened and are cooked: 3–4 minutes.

Heat the coconut oil in a large sturdy pan over a medium heat. Add the mustard seeds and fry for 30 seconds until they start to pop, then stir in the coconut and fry for 1 minute. Add the onion, ginger, garlic, green chillies and curry leaves and fry for a further 5 minutes.

Add the mussels and their liquor to the pan, followed by the fennel seeds, black pepper, garam masala, chilli powder, turmeric and salt. Cook for a further 1–2 minutes, then serve.

Mussels with lemongrass, chilli and kaffir lime leaves

SERVES 4

2 fat lemongrass stalks
1 tbsp sunflower oil
1–2 red bird's-eye
  chillies (depending
  how hot you like it),
  finely chopped
2 garlic cloves,
  finely chopped
3cm piece of fresh
  ginger, finely grated
2kg mussels, cleaned
  (see page 86)
2 x 200ml cartons
  coconut cream
2 fresh kaffir lime leaves
1 tbsp fish sauce
1 tbsp lime juice,
  or to taste
1 tsp sugar
A handful of Thai
  basil leaves
Lime wedges, to serve

Use coconut cream, not coconut milk, for intensity of flavour in this dish. I originally wrote this to be cooked on the barbecue, but it can just as easily be done on the top of the stove, in a wok or a large, deep saucepan.

Remove the outer layers from each lemongrass stalk, cut in half and set to one side. Chop the core finely. Place a flat-bottomed wok directly on the bars of the barbecue or on the side burner and, when hot, add the oil and the chopped lemongrass, chilli, garlic and ginger and cook briefly for about 30 seconds. Add the mussels, coconut cream, kaffir lime leaves and reserved lemongrass leaves, cover with a large lid and cook for 3–4 minutes, giving the mussels a quick stir halfway through, until they have all opened.

Uncover and stir in the fish sauce, lime juice, sugar and basil leaves. Divide between deep bowls and serve garnished with the lime wedges.

Clams with a garlic and nut picada

**SERVES 4 AS A
FIRST COURSE**
1kg small clams,
   such as carpetshell

For the picada
30g pine nuts
30g blanched almonds
25g slice crustless
   white bread
4 tbsp olive oil
4 garlic cloves
A small handful
   of flat-leaf parsley

Spanish picada consists of nuts, bread, garlic, olive oil and sometimes herbs, pounded together and used to thicken and flavour a sauce.

For the picada, heat a frying pan and dry-roast the pine nuts for 1 minute, the almonds for 2 minutes. Fry the bread in 2 tablespoons of the olive oil for 1 minute on each side until crisp. Break the fried bread into the bowl of a mini food processor, add the nuts and grind into a mixture like coarse sand. Add the garlic and parsley with the remaining oil and grind into a thick paste.

Wash the clams in plenty of cold water and discard any that don't show signs of closing when squeezed gently. Heat a large pan over a high heat, add the clams and 4 tablespoons water, cover and cook for 1–2 minutes, shaking the pan every now and then, until the clams have just opened.

Remove the pan from the heat, uncover and slightly tilt it so that you can pull the clams slightly away from the cooking liquor. Stir the picada into the cooking liquor to thicken it, then stir the mixture back through the clams. Serve straight away.

Clams with XO sauce, spring onions and coriander

SERVES 4 AS A
FIRST COURSE
3 tbsp vegetable oil
30g fresh ginger,
   grated or chopped
20g garlic (4 cloves),
   grated or chopped
1 fresh red chilli, thinly
   sliced (seeds removed
   if you want less heat)
2 tsp fermented black
   beans, chopped
1 tsp sugar
2 tbsp XO sauce
   (I like Lee Kum Kee)
1.5kg fresh clams or pipis,
   washed in cold water
2 tbsp Shaoxing wine
   or dry sherry
1 tbsp soy sauce
1 tbsp cornflour, slaked
   with a little water
6 spring onions, sliced
A handful coriander,
   roughly chopped

One of my favourite Chinese seafood dishes, particularly when made with Australian pipis. XO sauce is a spicy seafood sauce commonly used in southern China, and becoming increasingly available in the West. If the clams are straight out of the water they will produce a lot of liquid when they open. In this case, scoop out the clams and reduce the liquid by rapid boiling, then return the clams to the reduced sauce.

Heat the oil in a wok over a high heat. Add the ginger, garlic, chilli, black beans, sugar and XO sauce and sauté for 1–2 minutes.

Add the clams, Shaoxing wine and soy sauce, cover with a lid and cook over a high heat for 2 minutes, shaking the pan a couple of times. Check to see the clams are opened, then stir in enough of the cornflour to thicken the sauce to coat the back of a spoon.

Add the spring onions and coriander, toss a few times and serve.

Warm oysters with black beans, ginger and coriander

SERVES 4 AS A
FIRST COURSE
20 Pacific oysters
2.5cm fresh ginger,
    very finely chopped
7.5cm cucumber
1 tbsp chopped coriander
1 tsp chopped chives
1 tbsp Chinese
    fermented salted
    black beans, chopped
1 garlic clove,
    very finely chopped
1 tbsp dark soy sauce
2 tbsp dry sherry
4 tbsp sesame oil
Salt

Next to raw oysters in the shell, this is my favourite oyster dish. In Chinese restaurants they tend to cook the oysters comprehensively, but I like them just set.

Preheat the grill to high. Open the oysters as shown on page 91, and pour away half the liquor. Nestle the oysters on a heatproof platter covered in a thick layer of salt or in the grill pan so they can't roll over during cooking. Sprinkle each one with the chopped ginger and set aside.

Cut the cucumber into 2.5cm pieces, then cut each piece into matchsticks. Mix with the coriander and chives and set aside.

Put the black beans into a small pan with the garlic, soy sauce, sherry and sesame oil. Leave over a very low heat to warm through.

Grill the oysters for 3 minutes. Sprinkle a little of the cucumber mixture over each one. Spoon over a little of the sauce and serve immediately.

Baked scallops with guindilla pepper, chorizo and crisp breadcrumps

SERVES 4 AS A
FIRST COURSE
8 large prepared scallops
in the shell (see page 90)

For the sauce
5 dried guindilla peppers
or ½ tsp crushed dried
chilli flakes
4 tbsp olive oil
75g finely chopped shallot
4 garlic cloves, finely chopped
65g chorizo sausage, skinned
and finely chopped
1 Roasted red pepper
(see page 312),
finely chopped
2 medium tomatoes,
seeded and chopped
Sea salt and freshly
ground black pepper
60g breadcrumbs, from
day-old white bread
1 tsp pimentón
picante (smoked hot
Spanish paprika)

Inspired by the scallop dishes of Galicia in northern Spain, I've made a sauce of roasted red pepper, chorizo and soaked dried guindilla peppers. If you can't get hold of scallops in the shell, spoon the sauce into small baking dishes instead.

Remove the stalks from the dried peppers, slit them open and remove all the seeds. Soak in hot water for 1 hour. Drain, then scrape the flesh away from the skins with a spoon.

Preheat the oven to 200°C/gas 6.

Heat 3 tablespoons of the olive oil in a frying pan over a medium heat. Add the shallot, garlic and chorizo and cook gently, stirring occasionally, for 5 minutes or until the shallots are soft and sweet. Add the guindilla pepper flesh or chilli flakes, roasted red pepper and tomatoes, season with a little salt and simmer for another 3 minutes.

Detach the scallops from their shells and cut them horizontally in half, leaving the coral attached to one slice. Spoon some of the sauce into the bottom of each shell. Season the scallops lightly and place 2 slices, slightly overlapping, on the sauce. Mix the breadcrumbs and pimentón with the remaining olive oil and a pinch of salt and sprinkle over the top. Place side by side on a baking tray, and bake on the top shelf of the oven for 8–9 minutes or until the scallops are just cooked through and the breadcrumbs are crisp and golden. Serve at once.

Seared scallops with serrano ham

SERVES 4

8 thin slices of serrano ham
  or similar cured ham
Leaves from 1 frisée lettuce
  heart and a handful of
  other bitter salad leaves
50g chilled unsalted butter
12 prepared scallops
  (see page 90)
Salt and freshly ground
  black pepper
3 tbsp sherry vinegar
1 tbsp chopped parsley

I'm pleased that in Britain scallops are normally sold with the orange roe attached. Elsewhere it's often not the case and people are missing a treat, particularly in this timeless combination of seafood and cured ham.

Arrange the ham and a pile of the salad leaves on 4 plates. Generously rub the base of a large non-stick frying pan with the block of butter and cut the remainder into small pieces.

Set the pan over a high heat and, as soon as the butter starts to smoke, add the scallops and sear for 2 minutes on each side, seasoning them with a little salt and pepper as they cook. Arrange the scallops on top of the ham.

For the dressing, remove the pan from the heat, add the sherry vinegar and stir to scrape up any residue from the bottom of the pan. Return the pan to the heat, add a tablespoon of water and whisk in the butter, a few pieces at a time, then add the parsley and season with a little salt and pepper. Spoon the dressing over the leaves and serve.

Steamed scallops in the shell with ginger, soy, sesame oil and spring onions

SERVES 4

16 prepared scallops in
   the shell (see page 90)
1 tsp finely chopped
   fresh ginger
1 tbsp sesame oil
2 tbsp dark soy sauce
1 tbsp roughly
   chopped coriander
3 spring onions,
   thinly sliced

This is a favourite dish of mine from a good Chinese restaurant. I regard Chinese seafood cookery as among the best in the world.

Pour 2.5cm of water into the base of a wide shallow pan and bring it up to the boil. Loosen the scallops from their shells but leave them in place. Sprinkle each one with some of the ginger.

Arrange the scallops, in batches if necessary, on a petal steamer. Lower them into the pan, reduce the heat to medium, cover and cook for about 4 minutes until just set. Remove and keep warm while you cook the rest.

Meanwhile, put the sesame oil and soy sauce into a small pan and warm through.

Lift the scallops on to 4 warmed plates and pour over some of the warm soy sauce and sesame oil. Sprinkle over the coriander and spring onions and serve immediately.

Prawns with freshly grated coconut, green chillies and mustard seeds

SERVES 4-6

2 tbsp black mustard seeds

4–6 tbsp vegetable oil

1 medium onion, thinly sliced

1 tsp turmeric powder

250ml coconut milk

250g fresh or frozen coconut flesh, blitzed in a food processor or grated

1 tsp salt

350g peeled raw prawns (see page 68)

4 fresh green chillies, with seeds, cut lengthways into sixths

A handful of chopped coriander, to finish

A popular dish in Bengal, where both prawns and coconut abound. I suggest serving it, as in Bengal, as a little course on its own, but it's also delicious with rice and flatbreads.

Put the black mustard seeds into a mini food processor and add 2 tablespoons of water. Blend for a minute then add another 2 tablespoons water and continue blending until the seeds start to break up. Keep blending until you have a rough paste that resembles wholegrain mustard, adding a splash more water if needed. Set aside.

Heat the oil in a heavy-based saucepan over a low-medium heat. Add the onion and fry for 10 minutes. Add the blended mustard paste, turmeric, coconut milk, coconut flesh and salt. Bring to a boil then simmer for 4–5 minutes. Add the prawns and green chillies and simmer for a further 3–4 minutes until the prawns are pink and cooked through. Scatter with coriander and serve.

Prawn molee

A molee is a spicy seafood and coconut dish. When I first tasted this dish in Kerala, southern India, I remember thinking it could quite easily be a recipe from a very smart French restaurant, it was so delicate.

SERVES 4-6

2 tbsp coconut oil
¼ tsp ground black pepper
3 green cardamom pods,
    lightly bruised with
    a rolling pin
6 cloves
2 medium onions,
    thinly sliced
3 garlic cloves,
    thinly sliced
5cm fresh ginger,
    finely shredded
2 green chillies,
    slit lengthways,
    seeds removed
1 tsp salt
A small handful of
    fresh curry leaves
Small pinch (⅛ tsp)
    of turmeric powder
400ml coconut milk
1½ tsp toddy or white
    wine vinegar
500g large tail-on raw
    prawns (see page 68)
2 tomatoes, thinly sliced
    into rounds, to garnish
Boiled basmati rice,
    to serve

Heat the coconut oil in a heavy-based saucepan or karahi over a medium heat. Add the pepper, cardamoms and cloves and fry for 1 minute until fragrant. Add the onions and fry for 5 minutes until translucent, then stir in the garlic, ginger, chillies, salt and curry leaves and fry for 1 minute.

Add the turmeric, coconut milk and vinegar. Bring to a simmer and simmer for 4–5 minutes until reduced slightly, then add the prawns and simmer for a further 4 minutes until the prawns are cooked. Scatter the tomatoes on top, turn off the heat, cover the pan and set aside for 3–4 minutes. Serve with rice.

Grilled Dublin Bay prawns with a Pernod and olive oil dressing

See technique on page 73.

*Alternative seafood:
2 x 500g cooked lobsters,
halved, or large tiger prawns,
Morton Bay or Balmain bugs*

SERVES 4

16 large or 24 smaller
   cooked Dublin Bay prawns
   (langoustines)
2 small shallots, finely chopped
½ tbsp roughly chopped
   tarragon leaves
½ tbsp roughly chopped
   flat-leaf parsley leaves
1 tsp Dijon mustard
1 tsp dark soy sauce
90ml extra virgin olive oil
1½ tbsp lemon juice
1 tsp Pernod
50g butter, melted
Salt and freshly ground
   black pepper

This comes from Elizabeth David's *French Provincial Cooking*, where it's used for lobster; it works equally well with langoustines split in half or really big prawns.

Preheat the grill to high. Cut the Dublin Bay prawns open lengthways and scoop out the creamy contents of the heads and any red roe with a teaspoon. Put this into a small bowl and stir in the shallots, tarragon, parsley, mustard, soy sauce, oil, lemon juice, Pernod and a little salt and pepper to taste.

Place the halved prawns cut-side up on a baking tray or the rack of the grill pan and brush with the melted butter. Season lightly and grill for 1–2 minutes, until the shells as well as the meat are heated through. Serve the prawns with a little of the dressing spooned over, and the rest on the side for dipping.

Gremolata prawns

SERVES 4

1 large lemon
2 tbsp olive oil
20 unpeeled large
   raw prawns
Cayenne pepper (optional)
Coarse sea salt and freshly
   ground black pepper
3 garlic cloves, very
   finely chopped
4 tbsp chopped flat-leaf
   parsley leaves

Gremolata is, for me, the Italian equivalent of French persillade, which is parsley finely chopped with garlic.

Peel the zest off the lemon with a potato peeler. Pile the pieces up a few at a time and then cut them across into short thin strips.

Heat the oil in a large frying pan. Add the prawns and toss them over a high heat for 4–5 minutes, seasoning them with some cayenne pepper or black pepper and sea salt as you do so.

Cut the lemon in half and squeeze the juice from one half over the prawns. Continue to cook until the juice has almost evaporated – the prawns should be quite dry.

Take the pan off the heat and leave for about 1 minute to cool very slightly. Then sprinkle over the lemon zest, chopped garlic, parsley and ¼ teaspoon salt and toss together well. Pile the prawns into a large serving dish and serve with finger bowls and plenty of napkins.

Andalucian shrimp and spring onion fritters

Alternative seafood:
Australian school
prawns, shrimps

MAKES 16

300g whole raw unshelled
  small prawns or brown
  shrimps, or 175g raw
  peeled prawns
  (see page 68)
175g plain flour
½ tsp baking powder
Salt
300ml water
1 tbsp dry white wine
2 spring onions,
  thinly sliced
1 tbsp chopped flat-leaf
  parsley leaves
Olive oil, for shallow frying

It's perfectly OK to eat shrimps in the shell when they are made into a fritter and crisp-fried like this. You don't notice the shells as long as they are small; Falmouth Bay prawns during the autumn months, for example, would be ideal. But if you can't take it, use peeled raw prawns instead.

If using unshelled small prawns, such as those from Falmouth Bay, or brown shrimp, break off and discard the heads but leave the tails unpeeled. If using raw peeled prawns, cut them across into 5mm-thick slices.

Sift the flour, baking powder and a pinch of salt into a mixing bowl. Add the water and wine. Gradually mix the dry ingredients into the liquid to make a batter, then whisk until you have a thick cream. Fold in the prawns, spring onions and parsley.

Pour 5mm oil into a large frying pan and place over a high heat. Leave until hot and a drop of the batter sizzles immediately. Carefully drop large spoonfuls of the batter into the pan and spread each one out a little with the back of the spoon so they develop thin, crispy edges. Don't overcrowd the pan – only do 2–3 at a time. Cook, turning the fritters over every now and then, for about 2 minutes or until puffed up and golden brown on both sides.

Remove and drain on a tray lined with plenty of kitchen paper. Eat straight away while hot and crisp.

Potato gnocchi with prawns, tomato and basil

Alternative seafood: langoustines

SERVES 4

225g floury potatoes
80g flour
½ beaten egg (20g)
¼ tsp salt
2 medium tomatoes
300g large raw prawns
   in the shell
40ml extra virgin olive oil
2 small garlic cloves,
   finely chopped
150ml Chicken stock
   (see page 310)
A pinch of dried
   chilli flakes
A few fresh basil leaves,
   thinly sliced
Salt and freshly ground
   black pepper

I originally devised this dish to make use of the small, damaged but perfectly fresh langoustines we get at the Seafood Restaurant in Padstow. I use the shells to add flavour to an immediately made shellfish reduction, which becomes the sauce to go with the gnocchi and sliced tails.

Bake the potatoes until very tender, then leave to cool. Scoop out the flesh and mash it or pass it through a potato ricer. Blend with the flour, egg and salt into a firm mixture. Grab a handful of the mixture and roll it out until it is about 1cm thick. Cut this into 5mm 'pillows'. Do the same with the rest. Boil the gnocchi in salted water for 3–4 minutes.

Skin one of the tomatoes, remove the seeds and chop the flesh. Set this tomato concassé aside. Keep the seeds and skin.

Peel the prawns (see page 68) and slice the tail flesh into 1cm pieces. Keep the heads and shells: chop them up and put in a pan with half the olive oil, half the garlic, the other tomato roughly chopped, and the seeds and skins. Gently fry for about 3 minutes, then add the chicken stock, simmer for 10 minutes and reduce to about 40ml. Pass through a fine sieve, pressing out the liquid with the back of a ladle.

To finish, put the rest of the olive oil in a pan, add the rest of the garlic and the dried chilli. Add the sliced prawn tails and 1 tablespoon of the tomato concassé. Heat gently for about a minute just to set the prawns, then stir in the gnocchi. Add the sliced basil, season with salt and freshly ground black pepper and serve in pasta bowls with the sauce poured over.

Crab and Gruyère tartlets

SERVES 4
1 quantity Shortcrust
    pastry (see page 315)
2 eggs, separated
200g fresh white crab meat
50g fresh brown crab meat
90ml double cream
A pinch of cayenne pepper
Salt and freshly ground
    black pepper
50g Gruyère cheese,
    finely grated

One large cooked brown crab will supply the right amount of crab meat for these tarts.

Preheat the oven to 220°C/gas 7. Briefly knead the pastry on a lightly floured surface until smooth. Roll out and use to line 4 shallow 12cm loose-based tartlet tins. Chill for 20 minutes.

Line the pastry cases with baking paper and beans and bake blind for 15 minutes. Remove the paper and beans, brush the inside of each case with egg white and return to the oven for 2 minutes. Remove from the oven and lower the temperature to 200°C/gas 6.

Mix the crab meat with the egg yolks, cream, cayenne and some salt and pepper. Spoon the mixture into the tartlet cases and sprinkle with the Gruyère cheese. Bake at the top of the oven for 15–20 minutes, until lightly golden. Serve warm.

Crab with rocket, basil and lemon olive oil

SERVES 4

350g fresh hand-picked
    white crab meat
    (see pages 78–80)
2 tsp lemon juice
4 tsp Lemon olive oil
    (see page 312), plus
    extra for drizzling
8 basil leaves, finely shredded
A handful of wild rocket leaves
Sea salt and freshly ground
    black pepper, and cracked
    black pepper to garnish

A light, lively dish that brings out the very best of fresh white crab meat.

Put the crab meat into a bowl and gently stir in the lemon juice, lemon olive oil, basil and some seasoning to taste. Make a small, tall pile of the crab mixture on 4 plates, placing them slightly off centre. Put a small pile of rocket leaves alongside. Drizzle a little more olive oil over the rocket and around the outside edge of the plate, sprinkle the oil with a little sea salt and cracked black pepper and serve.

South-east Asian crab omelette with stir-fried vegetables

SERVES 4

For the nam prik sauce
Juice of 1 lime
1 large garlic clove
1 tbsp nam prik (Thai sweet
    chilli and shrimp sauce)
½ tsp sambal oelek
    (Indonesian red chilli paste)
25ml ketjap manis
    (sweet soy sauce)
100g palm sugar or light
    muscovado sugar
2 tbsp chopped coriander
1 tsp chopped mint

For the vegetable stir-fry
1 tbsp sunflower oil
40g fresh beansprouts
40g mangetout peas, shredded
½ red pepper, shredded
½ medium carrot, shredded
½ small red onion, thinly sliced
4 fresh shiitake mushrooms,
    thinly sliced
4 oyster mushrooms,
    torn into fine strips
15g Japanese pickled ginger,
    finely shredded

For the omelettes
4 tbsp sunflower oil
12 large eggs, beaten
225g fresh white crab meat
Sea salt and black pepper

Mud crabs come from the mangrove swamps of the northern part of Australia. They look a bit like European brown crabs, with equally powerful and dangerous claws. Any good fresh white crab meat will be fine for this recipe.

For the sauce, combine the lime juice and garlic in a blender or food processor until smooth. Add all the other ingredients and blend well. Add enough water to make a smooth, sauce-like consistency, then pass through a fine sieve.

For the vegetable stir-fry, heat the oil in a frying pan or wok, add all the vegetables and mushrooms and stir-fry for 1–2 minutes until just cooked but still crunchy. Add the pickled ginger and toss for a few seconds to heat through. Drizzle some of the nam prik sauce over each serving plate in a zigzag pattern and then put the stir-fried vegetables in the centre of each one.

For the omelettes, heat a 20–23cm omelette pan over a medium heat, add 1 tablespoon of the oil and, when it is hot, a quarter of the beaten eggs. Move the mixture over the base of the pan with the back of a fork until it begins to set, then stop stirring and cook until it is just a little moist on top – about 2 minutes in all. Put a quarter of the crab meat down the centre of the omelette and season to taste. Fold the omelette over twice and place on the stir-fried vegetables. Drizzle over a little more of the nam prik sauce and serve at once. Cook a further 3 omelettes in the same way.

Crab with wakame salad and wasabi mayonnaise

**SERVES 4 AS A
FIRST COURSE**
40g dried wakame seaweed
½ cucumber, peeled
225g fresh white crab meat
    (see pages 78–80)
1 tbsp bonito flakes

For the wakame dressing
½ tsp dashi granules
40ml warm water
8ml rice wine vinegar
½ tsp white sugar
1 tsp dark soy sauce

For the wasabi mayonnaise
2 egg yolks
2 tsp white wine vinegar
2 tsp wasabi paste
300ml rapeseed oil
½ teaspoon salt

This recipe comes from my Japanese period. It's a wonderful way of presenting beautiful white crab meat.

Drop the wakame into boiling water for 5 minutes, then drain well and slice if necessary.

Cut the cucumber in half lengthways and scoop out the seeds with a teaspoon. Cut across into thin slices.

For the wakame dressing, dissolve the dashi granules in the warm water and mix with the rest of the dressing ingredients. Add the wakame seaweed and the cucumber, and mix together well. Chill.

To make the mayonnaise, mix the egg yolks, white wine vinegar and wasabi paste together in a bowl. Using a wire whisk, gradually beat in the oil a few drops at a time, until you have incorporated it all. Season with the salt.

To serve, pile the crab meat on to 4 cold plates and put a tablespoon of the wasabi mayonnaise alongside. Put a handful of the cucumber and wakame seaweed next to the crab meat, sprinkle the bonito flakes on top of the seaweed, and serve.

Maryland crab cakes with a tarragon and butter sauce

See technique on page 81.

SERVES 4

500g fresh white crab meat

40g cream crackers or
saltines, finely crushed

1 egg

2 tbsp Mayonnaise
(see page 311), made
with sunflower oil

1 tbsp English
mustard powder

1 tbsp lemon juice

A dash of Worcestershire
sauce

Salt and freshly ground
white pepper

2 tbsp chopped parsley

4 tbsp Clarified butter
(see page 311)

*For the tarragon
and butter sauce*

50ml white wine vinegar

4 tbsp Clarified butter
(see page 311)

1 plum tomato, skinned,
seeded and diced

1 tsp chopped tarragon

Everywhere you go on the east coast of the USA you will find crab cakes. Two secrets to their making: use good crab and as little as possible of anything else; chill them for a good hour to firm them up before cooking.

Put the crab meat into a bowl and add just enough of the cracker crumbs to absorb any moisture. You may not need to add them all.

Break the egg into a small bowl and whisk in the mayonnaise, mustard, lemon juice, Worcestershire sauce and some seasoning. Fold this mixture into the crab meat, trying not to break up the lumps of crab. Stir in the parsley. Shape the mixture into eight 8cm patties, put them on a plate, cover with cling film and chill for at least 1 hour.

Heat the clarified butter in a large frying pan. Add the crab cakes (in 2 batches if necessary) and cook over a medium heat for 2–3 minutes on each side until crisp and richly golden.

For the sauce, boil the vinegar in a small pan until reduced to about 2 tablespoons. Add the clarified butter, tomato, tarragon and some salt and pepper and gently warm through. Serve with the crab cakes.

298 RECIPES | SHELLFISH

Singapore chilli crab

See technique on page 76.

Alternative seafood:
large raw prawns
or uncooked lobster

SERVES 4

2 x 900g live or cooked
    crabs
4 tbsp groundnut
    or sunflower oil
4 fat garlic cloves,
    finely chopped
2.5cm fresh ginger,
    finely chopped
4 tbsp tomato ketchup
3 medium-hot red
    chillies, finely chopped
2 tbsp dark soy sauce
150ml water
A few turns of the black
    pepper mill
2 spring onions, cut into
    5cm pieces and finely
    shredded lengthways

My life is measured out in memorable meals, and this, in Singapore, was one of them.

If using live crabs, kill them and prepare them for stir-frying (see page 76).

Heat the oil in a large wok. Add the crab pieces and stir-fry for 3 minutes, adding the garlic and the ginger after 1 minute.

Add about a quarter of the brown meat from the back shell, the tomato ketchup, red chillies, soy sauce, water and black pepper. Cover and simmer over a medium heat for 5 minutes if the crab is fresh or 2–3 minutes if using cooked crab. Serve the crab straight away with shredded spring onions scattered over.

Lobster thermidor

See technique on page 70.

Alternative:
make a seafood thermidor
by grilling whatever mixed
seafood you like – scallops,
prawns, crab – in a gratin
dish, sprinkled with
Parmesan, until brown.

SERVES 2
1 x 750g cooked lobster
25g butter
2 large shallots,
    finely chopped
600ml Fish stock
    (see page 310)
50ml Noilly Prat
75ml double cream
½ tsp English mustard
1 tsp chopped fines herbes
    (chervil, chives, parsley
    and tarragon)
1 tsp lemon juice
Salt and freshly ground
    black pepper
15g finely grated
    Parmesan cheese

Fifteen years ago the idea of putting precious lobster with a white wine sauce and sprinkling it with cheese would have been anathema to me, on the grounds that it smothered the taste. Now, influenced by my wife Sarah's addiction to it, I've quite changed my mind.

Remove the meat and any roe from the lobster (see the technique on page 70). Scoop out the head matter and set aside for the sauce. Cut the meat into small chunky pieces and return to the cleaned half-shells with any roe. Cover and set aside.

For the sauce, melt the butter in a small pan. Add the shallots and cook gently for 3–4 minutes until soft but not browned. Add the fish stock, Noilly Prat and half the double cream and boil until reduced by three-quarters to about 175ml. Add the rest of the cream and simmer until it has reduced to a good coating-sauce consistency. Whisk in the reserved head matter, the mustard, fines herbes and lemon juice. Season to taste.

Preheat the grill to high. Carefully spoon the sauce over the lobster meat and sprinkle lightly with Parmesan cheese. Grill for 2–3 minutes until golden and bubbling.

Lobster with ginger, spring onions and soft egg noodles

Alternative seafood: crab, prawns

SERVES 2-3

1 x 750g live lobster or
    spiny lobster (crayfish)
Sunflower oil, for deep-
    frying, plus 1 tbsp
1 tsp salt
½ tsp sugar
1 tbsp dark soy sauce
1 tbsp oyster sauce
A pinch of freshly ground
    white pepper
1 tsp toasted sesame oil
2 tbsp rice wine or dry sherry
2 tbsp cornflour
2 garlic cloves, crushed
120g fresh ginger, thinly
    sliced on a mandolin
90g spring onions,
    cut into 2.5cm pieces
250ml Chicken stock
    (see page 310)
175g fresh egg thread noodles

This recipe came from the Mandarin Kitchen in Queensway, London. It's one of my favourite Chinese seafood dishes.

Prepare the lobster for stir-frying (see page 74). Heat some oil for deep-frying to 190°C. Mix the salt, sugar, dark soy sauce, oyster sauce, white pepper, sesame oil and rice wine or sherry together in a small bowl and set aside. Bring a large pan of water to the boil for the noodles.

Sprinkle the lobster pieces with 1½ tablespoons of the cornflour and deep-fry, in 2 or 3 batches if necessary, for 2 minutes. The larger claw might take longer – about 3 minutes. Lift out and drain on kitchen paper.

Heat the tablespoon of sunflower oil in a wok. Add the garlic, ginger and spring onions and stir-fry for a few seconds. Add the lobster to the wok with the soy sauce mixture and stir-fry for 1 minute. Add the chicken stock, then cover and cook over a medium heat for 2 minutes.

Drop the noodles into the pan of boiling water, cover and remove from the heat. Soak for 2 minutes, loosening them now and then with chopsticks or a fork.

Mix the rest of the cornflour with 2 tablespoons cold water, add to the wok and stir for 1 minute, until the sauce thickens.

Drain the noodles, spoon the lobster mixture on top and serve straight away.

Lobster raviolo with basil and spinach

Alternative seafood: prawns or crab meat (to save on cost). You need about 45g lobster per person so use that amount of prawn or crab meat instead (180g total).

SERVES 4 AS A
FIRST COURSE

For the pasta dough
75g strong flour
25g semolina
2 medium eggs
A pinch of salt

*For the lobster and
   mousseline filling*
550g cooked whole lobster
350g skinned fillets of
   cheap flatfish such as
   plaice, flounder or dab
1 medium egg
2 tsp lemon juice
¾ tsp salt
300ml double cream

For the sauce
600ml Fish stock
   (see page 310)
85ml double cream
50g unsalted butter
85ml dry white wine
A few basil leaves,
   thinly sliced

12 spinach leaves,
   preferably small ones

Raviolo in the singular: just one big one per person. This dish is designed to make a small amount of lobster go a long way, but it is still very much a luxury first course.

Mix together the ingredients for the pasta dough and knead until smooth. Leave to rest for 20 minutes before rolling and cutting. If you have a pasta machine, roll the dough to setting number 6. If you don't, roll out to no more than 2mm thick. Using a 12cm cutter or a bowl, cut out 8 discs.

Remove the meat from the lobster (see page 70) and slice it into 5mm slices. If there is any coral in the lobster, cut it up and add with all the brown meat from the lobster's head.

Put the fish fillet, egg, lemon juice and salt and 150ml of the double cream into a food processor. Blend until smooth, then pour in the rest of the cream in a steady stream taking only about 10 seconds; any longer and the mixture will curdle.

Pile the mousseline and lobster meat in the centre of each of 4 of the pasta discs, leaving a 1cm border. Moisten the outer edge of each disc with water. Put the 4 remaining discs on top, slide a palette knife under each raviolo and place on the palm of your hand. Gently crimp the edges together with your fingers, pulling the disc round as you do.

Drop the ravioli into a large pan of boiling salted water for about 40 seconds. Remove and place on a tray. You can make these ravioli a day in advance. Cover with cling film and store in the fridge.

To serve, rapidly boil the fish stock, cream, butter and white wine together until the sauce has reduced to the point where it will coat the back of a spoon. Stir in the basil and keep warm.

Bring a pan of salted water to the boil, drop in the spinach leaves and blanch briefly for about 20 seconds. Remove and keep warm. Put the ravioli in the same water, reduce the heat and poach for 4–5 minutes. Take 4 warmed plates and lay the spinach leaves out in the centre. Put a raviolo on top and spoon the sauce over.

Cover the slice of bread with the stock or water and leave to soften. Squeeze out the excess liquid and put the bread into a food processor with the harissa, garlic, egg yolk and salt. Blend until smooth. With the machine still running, gradually add the oil until you have a smooth, thick, mayonnaise-like mixture. Keeps in the fridge for at least a week.

ROASTED RED PEPPER
Spear the stalk end of a red pepper on a fork and turn the pepper in the flame of a gas burner or blowtorch until the skin has blistered and blackened. Alternatively, roast the pepper in a hot oven at 220°C/gas 7 for 20–25 minutes, turning once, until the skin is black. Remove the pepper from the heat and leave to cool. Break it in half and remove the stalk, skin and seeds. The flesh is ready to use.

HARISSA
1 Roasted Red Pepper
  (see above)
1 tsp tomato purée
1 tsp ground coriander
A pinch of saffron strands
2 medium-hot red Dutch
  chillies, stalks removed
  and roughly chopped
¼ tsp cayenne pepper
¼ tsp salt

Put all the ingredients into a food processor and blend until smooth.

CHIPOTLE RELISH
200g onions, chopped
30g garlic, chopped
30ml vegetable oil
15g chipotle chilli
400g canned tomato
3 tbsp tomato purée

2 tsp salt
240ml malt vinegar
120g sugar
200ml water

Cook the onions and garlic in the oil for 10 minutes over a medium heat. Add all the other ingredients and cook very gently for 45 minutes until quite thick. Transfer to a sterilized jar unless using immediately.

SLOW-COOKED GARLIC
Makes 1 jar
125g garlic cloves,
  roughly chopped
100ml olive oil
¼ tsp salt

It is a lot easier to control the caramelization of garlic when it is cooked in a large quantity in lots of olive oil. Put the garlic and olive oil into a small pan and cook over a very gentle heat for 20 minutes, stirring every now and then, and mashing it up with a potato masher after about 15 minutes, until the garlic is soft and sweet. Season with the salt, leave to cool, then spoon into a container with a lid and refrigerate. Keeps for 2–3 weeks.

LEMON OLIVE OIL
Pare the zest from 1 lemon with a potato peeler. Cut the zest into thin strips and stir into 600ml extra virgin olive oil. Leave to infuse for 24 hours before using.

TAPENADE
75g pitted black olives,
  drained and rinsed
4 anchovy fillets in olive
  oil, drained
25g capers, drained
  and rinsed

3 garlic cloves
75ml olive oil
Freshly ground black pepper

Put the olives, anchovies, capers and garlic into a food processor and pulse 3 or 4 times. Then turn the processor on and add the oil in a thin steady stream. Season with black pepper, spoon into a sterilized glass jar and seal. Keeps in the fridge for up to 3 months.

TOSA SAUCE
250ml soy sauce
5cm piece kombu
3 tbsp mirin
A small handful of dried
  bonito flakes

Soak all the ingredients for 24 hours, then strain. Keeps for up to a year.

TAMARIND WATER
Makes 150ml
Take a piece of tamarind pulp about the size of a tangerine and put it in a bowl with 150ml warm water. Work the paste into the water with your fingers until it has broken down and the seeds have been released. Strain through a fine sieve into another bowl and discard the fibrous material left in the sieve. The water is now ready to use. Keeps in the fridge for 24 hours.

CHAT MASALA
Makes 50–75g
1 tbsp cumin seeds
1 tbsp coriander seeds
1 tbsp black peppercorns
1 tbsp amchur (dried green
  mango powder)
1 tbsp dried ginger powder
1 tsp asafoetida

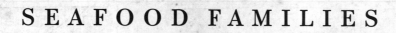

SEAFOOD FAMILIES

octopus are found on the Eastern Seaboard of America, north of the Carolinas.

The general rule of thumb is: the smaller the species, the more tender it will be. With the exception of octopus, they need to be cooked quickly so that they remain so – no more than 1 minute in a hot pan – after which time they tend to toughen and then you should slow-cook them in the same way as octopus (see page 94) to render them tender again.

Squid

To me the taste of squid is of pure seafood. Nothing is more exciting than the smell of fresh squid cooking quickly in hot olive oil, or in a wok with the attendant aromas of garlic and ginger, in somewhere like the Seafood Restaurant in Bangkok. Squid is popular everywhere now. It should be cooked for the briefest time, in the hottest oil or grilled, baked, or stir-fried (see pages 114 and 250). I don't enjoy the taste of boiled squid so, for a fish stew, I add it fried at the last minute.

There is a theory that frozen squid are as good as fresh, but I don't find this to be so. Freezing seems to make them tougher and remove most of their taste but, like all frozen seafood, the quality depends more on the length of time they have been frozen than any deterioration caused by the rapid drop in temperature. Cuttlefish is also becoming more popular, though it tends to be a little tougher than squid.

Octopus

The Common Octopus (*Octopus Vulgaris*) has two rows of suckers on each tentacle. It is the best species for eating as it only needs to be simmered for 45 minutes to 1 hour in salted water to tenderize it, and there's no need for any bashing, freezing or dunking in boiling water.

The species generally caught in UK waters is the Lesser curled or horned octopus (*Eledone cirrhosa*). This species also occurs in the Mediterranean. It only

has single rows of suckers and needs to be cooked a lot longer or tenderized by breaking down the muscle structure.

COD AND COD-LIKE FISH
Cod

In one of my earlier books I included a recipe for Crab Newburg by Marjorie Kinnan Rawlings, which ends 'I sit alone and weep for the misery of a world that does not have blue crabs and a Jersey cow', to which list I would add, cod.

The world cries out for a thick, white flaky fillet of fish, not assertive in flavour and not filled with bones, and cod is that fish. The fact that it is fished out on the Grand Banks of the US Eastern Seaboard and virtually fished out in the North Sea has, more than anything, drawn attention to the alarming reduction in fish stocks everywhere. I recall people saying that cod was bland and boring but it only takes a shortage to concentrate the mind on appreciating one of the best fish in the sea.

Anyone with even a passing interest in fish should read Mark Kurlansky's book *Cod*. In it you will discover that the cod along the Grand Banks in the US were once so plentiful that they could be gathered simply by dropping weighted baskets over the sides of the boats and lifting them, brimming with fish, back up through the shoals.

As a colourful illustration of the fecundity of cod, and the appalling cack-handedness of our attempts to preserve the species, through our greed and political expediency, I enjoy this quote by Alexander Dumas in *Le Grand Dictionnaire*, 1873. 'It has been calculated that if no accident prevented the hatching of the eggs, and each egg reached maturity, it would take only three years to fill the sea, so that you could walk across the Atlantic dry shod on the backs of cod.'

There are still stocks of the smaller but similar PACIFIC COD that is marketed as TRUE COD on the west

coast of America to distinguish it from various other unrelated fish that are sold as cod. This problem is prevalent in Australia and New Zealand too – testimony perhaps to the worldwide demand for the characteristic clean taste of this prized fish.

Fortunately, the Norwegians and Icelanders have long practised sensible conservation of cod stocks off their coasts, and much of the world's cod come from these cold waters. Though the records of enormous cod weighing 50kg or more are now mere historical facts, you can still buy 5–6kg fish, which are fantastic eating. Fish of this size are normally sold in fillets and a portion brushed with butter, sprinkled with sea salt and cracked black pepper and grilled is as good as cod gets. Wherever possible, therefore, go for thick fillets.

Small cod up to 1kg, known as CODLING in Europe and SCROD in America, are nice to eat if fresh but don't have the superb falling-away flaky texture of the bigger fish. Cod when it's just caught is quite tough, and while I love this chewiness, some prefer to leave it a day or two until the flesh goes through the same enzymatic change as meat and becomes more tender.

Preserved cod

Historically, far more cod was consumed salted because of lack of refrigeration, but even today the demand for SALT COD, BACALAO, and dried cod (STOCKFISH) is enormous. Properly soaked – over a couple of days – and then poached and served with some sympathetic flavours such as garlic, tomato and olive oil – it is real comfort food for the Spanish, Portuguese, Italians and French. I recently had a carpaccio of salt cod where the salt cod had been soaked for sufficiently long to remove any trace of salt and was then served raw and thinly sliced with San Marzano tomatoes, rocket and extra virgin olive oil. Accompanied by a glass of Greco di Tufo, the versatility of this ancient way of curing cod was brought home to me.

Haddock

This, the next most popular member of the cod family, has also suffered from serious over-fishing. It's just as good as cod and, while it lacks the whiteness and beautiful flakes of that fish, it has a slightly sweeter flavour. Again, it is best in thick fillets, but it's not as big a fish as cod, weighing on average 2–3kg. In Britain a great deal of rather small fish is landed, especially owing to the preference for haddock over cod in the fish-and-chip shops of the north. But I think they are rather unsuited to being battered and deep-fried because they dry out.

Smoked haddock

Of all the cod family, haddock is best for smoking due to its slightly sweet flavour. All haddock-fishing countries have a range of smoked haddock specialities. In Britain, FINNAN HADDOCK is traditionally smoked over peat while ARBROATH SMOKIES are small whole haddock, hot-smoked over pits of smouldering oak. In Europe, Denmark produces some good-quality smoked haddock, as does France where it is called 'haddock' to distinguish it from the fresh fish or *églefin*.

In the United States smoked haddock comes from Boston and Portland, Maine, while the smoked haddock or cod on sale in fishmongers in Australia and New Zealand will have come from either northern Europe or North America.

Hake

Of the rest of the cod family, hake is the most far-flung species appearing not only in the North Atlantic, Mediterranean and North Pacific, but also as far south as New Zealand, as the SOUTHERN HAKE, and *Merluccius australis*. A very similar species, *Merluccius capensis*, is currently the prime target of a massive European fishery off the coast of South Africa. In Europe, the Spanish are by far and away the biggest consumers of hake in the world and, like them, I find it hard to see why it's not more popular in

America and Australasia. It has a beguiling soft texture and good flavour and, I think, takes to butter or cream better than any other fish, except for turbot or brill. It is also rather good served cold with mayonnaise or sauce verte, which is an olive-oil mayonnaise with blanched spinach, rockets and herbs blitzed into it.

Whiting

Whiting is extensively fished in Northern Europe. It's not the best flavoured of the cod family, but small fish cooked whole – particularly deep-fried 'en colère' (see page 148) – are a delight.

Ling, forkbeard, white hake and pollack

I would describe all the rest of the cod family as lesser species as they don't have the same commercial appeal. All LING are firm textured with a mild, delicate flavour. I've had some success cooking fillets of our British ling on a charcoal grill. There is a species similar to ling in the Mediterranean – it's called the FORKBEARD and is usually cooked in the same way as hake – and also a couple in North America, the WHITE HAKE (also called the BOSTON LING) and the SQUIRREL HAKE.

Like hake, ling appears not just in the North Atlantic but also in the South Pacific as PINK LING and ROCK LING POLLACK, not to be confused with the North American 'POLLOCK', which is actually coley, and is quite a good substitute for cod. Pollack doesn't grow as big as cod, its average size being 2–3kg, but a fillet taken from a larger fish and grilled is almost as good as the real thing.

Coley, cusk and pouting

Also known as SAITHE, POLLOCK or COALFISH, COLEY has quite a good flavour but is let down by its dull grey colour on the slab, some of which remains after cooking. It can be substituted for either cod or haddock in any recipe and makes very good fish cakes. The flesh of TUSK, or CUSK, as it is more commonly known in America,

is rather oilier than most *Gadidae* (members of the cod family) and is therefore best grilled or baked. POUTING or POUT is a cheap member of the cod family that doesn't keep well. Rather a dull, light brown in colour with a very fragile fillet, it is best used in fish cakes or fish pies and is most similar to whiting. It has bulbous eyes, which seem to expand when trawled up from any great depth, testimony to the fact that fish brought up from the deep suffer, as we do, from the 'bends'.

CRUSTACEANS

Crabs

The meat of all crabs is fairly similar in taste all over the world, with each region asserting that theirs is the best. So I have simply organized them by size – small, medium and large.

Small crabs

The very smallest of crabs are called OYSTER or PEA CRABS. I once received a letter from a woman who had watched me prepare mussels on one of my television programmes. In it she warned me of the need to clean mussels on the inside, as well as the outside, because of the poisonous little crabs that live inside the shell of mussels and oysters. I've heard of this anxiety before, but actually these crabs are perfectly edible, and some oyster-shucking houses in the US used to sell them as a valuable by-product, for deep-frying or adding to soups.

The GREEN CRAB or SHORE CRAB weighs no more than 10g, but it has a ready market in Europe for such soups as the Shore Crab Bisque, on page 107. We have had success gathering them when soft-shelled, dipping them in tempura batter and serving them with a dipping sauce of chilli, lime and nam pla (Thai fish sauce).

The SWIMMING CRAB or VELVET CRAB, called the ETRILLE by the French, is surprisingly full of sweet, fibrous meat. I once ate a plate of them in Spain and noted that there was a distinction made between the local Velvet Crabs (called NECORA) and those described as 'foreign', which presumably come from Cornwall, and fetch a lower price. I must say I couldn't tell the difference.

Of all the small crabs, the one which grabs the most praise is the BLUE CRAB from the Eastern Seaboard of the United States, which reaches sizes of up to 200g. Whether in its hard shell or in its all-edible soft-shell form, it seems to have a higher ratio of lumpy exquisite meat than any other. Would that in the UK we could buy tubs of fresh white crab meat as you can in Chesapeake Bay.

Medium crabs
The crab most similar to the BLUE CRAB, but of medium size, is the ASIAN BLUE SWIMMER, *Portunus pelagicus*, of Australia. It is ideal for stir-frying in the shell, as it's easy to pick out the chunky, fibrous meat, and it's the best choice for Singapore Chilli Crab (see page 298). The other major crab from Australia and New Zealand is the MUD CRAB (MANGROVE CRAB), which has a much thicker shell and incredibly powerful claws. It much more resembles the European BROWN CRAB and the DUNGENESS CRAB of the northern Pacific, but is also very closely related to the excellent flavoured SAND CRAB of the Carolinas and Florida in the US. Another excellent flavoured crab, with pink-tinged meat, from America is the RED CRAB. It lives on the outer continental shelf at depths of between 350 and 2,000 metres.

Naturally I consider the brown crab to be second to none for flavour but possibly the European SPIDER CRAB has the most scented flavour of all crabs. The similar-looking SNOW CRAB in America has rather coarser, yellowish meat with good flavour.

Large crabs
One of the two most spectacular large crabs is the ALASKAN KING CRAB which can weigh up to 10kg. These are sold as crabmeat, rarely as whole crabs

because their enormous size and the fact that they are fished for off Alaska would make bringing the whole crab to market uneconomical.

The largest crab in the world is the KING CRAB from southern Australia and Tasmania, which can weigh up to 17kg, though the normal market size is about half that. These are favoured by the Chinese communities of Australian cities, where they are often kept spectacularly on show in tanks at the front of the restaurant.

Lobster
A trip to New England, USA and the pleasure of eating lobster rolls at Bob's Clam House showed that in some favoured parts of the world, lobster need not be the frighteningly expensive luxury it is where I come from. Lobster rolls are simply lobster meat in a slightly sweet finger bun with mayonnaise – now that's fast food I approve of!

Lobster is the world's most sought-after seafood. Its firm, sweet, white meat is satisfyingly full of flavour, and the flavour of all lobsters is remarkably similar the world over. The question of which country's lobsters are the best is easily answered for me. Wherever you can get one straight from the sea and cooked on the spot, that's the place where the best one will be. Lobsters deteriorate very quickly after death, so they have to be kept alive in a recirculation tank called a vivarium. But they can't be fed in them because this would contaminate the water and they would die. Unfortunately, the relatively small amount of water in which they live while in these tanks can affect their flavour. This explains why a lobster at the Seafood Restaurant in Padstow, straight out of the Atlantic and grilled with a little butter and chopped fines herbes, or cooked and served just with mayonnaise, will always taste better than one eaten in London.

The only lobsters with significant claws, the EUROPEAN and AMERICAN LOBSTERS, come from the North Atlantic. The American lobster is slightly

larger than the European and is dark green when alive, whereas the European one is blue. The claws of the American lobster are more rounded and, when cooked, it has a more orange hue than the European one, but in both cases the best sizes are 500g–1kg.

Lobsters with claws tend to prefer cold water though they can be found as far south as the Mediterranean and South Carolina. SPINY LOBSTERS (CRAYFISH), on the other hand, occur both in the southern hemisphere and northern hemisphere, as far north as Norway. They grow a lot bigger than true lobsters but I still think that the best size is 500g–2kg. The most obvious difference between them and the true lobster is the absence of any claws, but they are cooked in the same way and make just as good eating. My preference is for the WESTERN ROCK LOBSTER from western Australia.

Similar to spiny lobsters are various FLAT or SLIPPER LOBSTERS of Europe, called cigales. This is the French word for cicada, and refers to the cricket-like noises that they make underwater. With typical Australian bluntness, these slipper lobsters are known there as bugs, notably the BALMAIN BUG and MORETON BAY BUG. In the USA the similar species are known as SHOVEL-NOSED or SPANISH LOBSTERS or, echoing the French name, LOCUST LOBSTER. All these species are good eating though, due to a tendency to dryness, I find them far better if slightly undercooked. Incidentally, there is no danger in eating raw or undercooked lobster, as the splendour of thinly sliced lobster sashimi will testify. As with spiny lobsters, the meat of slipper lobsters is all in the tail.

If you find you have bought a lobster with soft, woolly flesh, it will be because it has been cooked after it has died. On death, the flesh of both lobsters and crabs goes through a rapid enzyme change, which reduces it almost to pulp within a couple of hours. The only ways to prevent this with lobster are either to remove the tail and claws from the head on death, or rapidly freeze it. Although I have classed DUBLIN BAY PRAWNS as large prawns, they are more closely related to lobsters and in the USA are called LOBSTERETTES. They also suffer from this rapid deterioration on death, which is why cooked langoustines can so often be disappointing.

Prawns and shrimps
Until it became easy in Britain to buy PRAWNS from America (called SHRIMPS there), Asia and Australia, cooked prawn dishes were relatively rare, simply because our native shrimps and prawns are small and don't suit grilling, pan-frying, barbecuing or deep-frying. We do have great dishes such as prawn cocktail or potted shrimps but generally a pile of cooked prawns and shrimps was something to peel at leisure and eat with a bowl of mayonnaise and some brown bread and butter.

There are really only three main types of prawns or shrimps native to Britain. The BROWN SHRIMP, caught off the coast of East Anglia and in Morecambe Bay in Lancashire, have a beautiful ephemeral flavour and should be eaten immediately after being boiled in seawater. I like to think of them as the seafood equivalent of violets in spring. They are also the sine qua non of potted shrimps, the superb delicacy that is thankfully still alive and well in Morecambe. The PINK SHRIMP or COMMON PRAWN is excellent but difficult to get hold of unless you live near the coast. I like to eat the larger ones just with mayonnaise but the smaller ones are great in a seafood risotto (see page 115). Finally, the NORTH ATLANTIC PRAWN is the must have type for a prawn cocktail.

The other common prawn available on sale everywhere in Britain is the MEDITERRANEAN PRAWN or CREVETTE, which I think is best served whole with mayonnaise or aïoli, the garlic mayonnaise from Provence (see page 311). I really like to squeeze the roe out of the heads of these prawns

– it's delicious and a treat missed by most people.

Now though it's easy to get large prawns, so dishes such as Prawn Molee (page 276) and Prawn Caldine (page 280) are easy to make in Britain. But imported prawns are still rather unhelpfully labelled as just small, medium or large, raw or cooked. Sometimes they're called by their correct name, such as BLACK TIGER PRAWNS, but I look forward to a time when we can enjoy the subtle differences of prawns as found in Australia.

In America you'll find the luxurious ROYAL RED SHRIMP from the Gulf of Mexico, with its deep red colour even when raw, and the CARIBBEAN (GULF) WHITE SHRIMP, which is the best-eating shrimp in the country, found from North Carolina down to the Gulf of Mexico and Texas. On the Pacific coast the SIDE-STRIPE SHRIMP, the PINK SHRIMP and the COON-STRIPE SHRIMP are also, like prawns in the UK, just referred to as shrimp – small, medium and large – and not by their individual names.

In Australia, the BANANA PRAWN is known for its sweet, moist and medium-firm texture, while the KING PRAWN can reach up to 30cm in length. The BAY PRAWN is only ever sold locally where it's caught and, though fetching less money than other prawns, is much sought after because of its seasonality.

Dublin Bay prawns,
scampi or langoustine
With their rather important-sounding name of *Nephrops norvegicus*, these are the crowning glory of prawns in the UK. They can grow up to 250g in weight, at which size they look like small lobsters and they are in fact a member of the lobster family. Generally I prefer to eat them as they are, served in their shell. But a very simple way to serve cooked langoustine hot is to cut them in half, brush them with melted butter and grill them briefly. Serve them with hot melted butter and lemon juice. You can add some finely chopped fines herbes

(chervil, chives, parsley and tarragon) to the butter if you like. A similar species found on the same sort of ground off the coast of Scotland is the SQUAT LOBSTER. Species very like our langoustine are also found in the USA, Australia and New Zealand.

DEEP-SEA FISH
This is of course not a family of fish, but rather a group in which all the species have a sort of similarity, conditioned by the dark depths in which they live. For the most part this means they have enormous eyes with which to catch what little light there is, and generally, possibly due to the decompression when raising them to the surface, they look wan and flabby.

The PATAGONIAN TOOTHFISH, also known as the CHILEAN SEA BASS or ANTARCTIC SEA BASS, comes from the southern oceans of the world, around South Georgia in the Falklands and off the bottom of South America. It always comes in skinned fillets and though not related to bass at all, it can be cooked in much the same way. There is considerable concern, though, about the long-term stability of stocks of this fish. Like all deep-water fish, there are no restrictions on the fishing of them as they are outside territorial waters.

Other prize fish from these depths are the ORANGE ROUGHY and HOKI (BLUE GRENADIER), though the grenadier, with the other unfortunate name of RAT-TAIL, also provides firm, meaty fillets. The orange roughy is sometimes available fresh in Australia and New Zealand and can be extremely good, but generally it is sold as skinned and de-fatted fillets, frozen at sea, which need a lot of nurturing during cooking to make them interesting.

Other interestingly named and curiously shaped deep-water fish are the RABBITFISH from the Atlantic, the ALFONSINO, and the RIBALDO from the southern Pacific. Alfonsino are abundant in the Pacific Ocean and are very popular in China, where they're known as POH LAP, and Japan, where they're called MADAI. They have thick scaly skin and white, slightly oily flesh and should be prepared like sea bream. Ribaldo also carries the name of DEEP-SEA COD. While this produces thick fillets of fish, it has soft flesh and should be eaten quickly before it deteriorates.

DRUMS

DRUMS and CROAKERS in the USA and the MULLOWAY of Australia are all members of the *Sciaenidae* family. These are distinguished by having an internal muscle that is used to beat the swim bladder, producing a sound described as either a drumming or croaking that can sometimes even be heard from land. By far the greatest variety of species occurs in America. On the east coast the best eating varieties are the WEAKFISH and the RED DRUM. The weakfish weighs on average between 500g and 3kg. They are either sold whole or in fillets and have white, sweet and finely textured flesh. The flesh is fragile and the fish needs to be iced quickly after capture. The roes are particularly well flavoured too. Weakfish and a closely related fish, the SPOTTED SEA TROUT (also known as the SPOTTED SQUETEAGUE), are often just called trout in the southern States, which can be confusing to those used to the fish of the salmon family. Highly regarded relations of the weakfish and spotted sea trout are the CORVINAS of Central America.

RED DRUM, caught along the south Atlantic and Gulf coasts, has moist, white and heavy-flaked flesh. The best drums from the Pacific are the WHITE SEABASS from California and the SILVER PERCH, which only grows to about 1kg in size and is therefore a tasty, pan-sized fish. On the east coast there's also the ATLANTIC CROAKER, which has lean white meat, and the TOTUAVA, the largest of the drums, which is always sold in steak form for grilling or barbecuing.

Mulloway
Similar species to the drums occur in Australia with the MULLOWAY, the DHUFISH (incorrectly known in the past as the CROAKER or DRUM) and the BLACK DHUFISH (previously known as the SPOTTED CROAKER). These are large fish, common on both eastern and western coasts, and usually sold in fillet form. I find the flesh of the mulloway similar in texture to sea bass, though they are not related, and I often recommend it when suggesting alternative fish. It's not a commercial fish, being regarded more as a prestige angling fish.

EEL AND EEL-LIKE FISH
It is small wonder that the FRESHWATER EEL turns up looking remarkably similar all the world over, when you consider the enormous distances they migrate from the world's seas to rivers, and back again. The EUROPEAN EEL, *Anguilla anguilla*, and the AMERICAN EEL, *Anguilla rostrata*, are both born in the Sargasso Sea, east of Florida and, as ELVERS, spend three years swimming to Europe or one year swimming to America. The freshwater eels of Australia and New Zealand, the LONGFIN EEL and SHORTFIN EEL, are born in the Coral Sea and take a year to swim to the rivers of Eastern Australia and New Zealand.

The eating qualities of eel fall into the three distinct eras in their lives. As elvers, they can fetch a small fortune during the short European season in early March. They are served up by the Spanish in tiny, piping-hot cazuelas with olive oil and garlic. The elvers that get away grow into browny-yellow adult eels and it is in this phase that most of them are caught. Then, as they start their journey back to the Sargasso Sea to spawn and die, they become more pointed. Having become very fatty they now stop eating and become sleeker and silvery, ready for the change of habitat on the long voyage home. These SILVER EELS are the best eating and favoured by eel smokers for

their quality and delicious fat content. Indeed it is the fattiness of eels that makes them so special – it is of a purity and tastiness unequalled. The Chinese are masters of eel cooking. Sadly in the UK all eels, particularly the juvenile elvers, are now regarded as under threat.

Moray eel
The other two main types of eel are the Mediterranean MORAY EEL and the CONGER EEL. Moray Eel is much sought after, being firm and almost like Dover sole in quality. There's a mosaic from Pompeii in the National Archaeological Museum in Naples, Italy, which shows a selection of the Romans' best-loved Mediterranean fish, including the yellow-speckled moray eel. And it still looks as fresh and ready to be cooked as if it had been caught yesterday. It is a superb fish, firm-fleshed and fresh tasting and so much more interesting than the CONGER EEL.

Conger eel
This appears all over the world in slightly different forms. It's a big, fierce beast and generally caught on a line. Few seem to cook it except for Europeans – notably the northern Spanish, the Bretons of France and the Cornish. It's a common ingredient in bouillabaisse and the fish stew cotriade from Brittany. We often use it in our Classic Fish Soup (see page 102). I once created a recipe for a pot roast or Poêle of Conger of which I'm still very fond. I wrap the eel in a pig's caul and cook it in a heavy-lidded casserole with root vegetables.

Lamprey
A brief mention must also be made of this eel-like fish that inhabits the estuarine waters of northern Europe. It also lives in American waters but it's not esteemed, possibly because of its rather horrifying way of feeding. It attaches itself to another fish with the sucking disc, which it has instead of a mouth, bores a hole through the skin with its rasp-like teeth and sucks

the blood out. Which, incidentally, doesn't always kill the fish. You sometimes catch a fish, particularly salmon, with a lamprey scar on it. The classic lamprey dish is Lamproie à la Bordelaise, where it is stewed in red wine. Lampreys have no scales and their bones are more like the cartilage in a shark.

ELONGATED FISH

There is, of course, no such scientific family as elongated fish but it seemed an apt grouping of fish that stand out in markets all over the world by virtue of their sinuousness, and which are all treated in much the same way.

Barracuda

All barracuda (and there are about six types found in temperate and tropical waters around the world) are what I call medium quality fish: firm, mild-flavoured, with a medium fat content. Because the fish are big, they are free from irritating small bones and are commonly sold in fillet form or in steaks. But beware, barracuda spoils quickly, so cook it within 24 hours of buying it. Because they're not fantastically well flavoured, they are ideal in robust dishes such as fish curries and habanero-chilli-hot Caribbean dishes. Apart from their eating qualities, they are thoroughly interesting fish. Fierce streamlined killers, they have the most amazing array of needle-like teeth, each one of which has its own hole on the opposing jaw, allowing the barracuda to close its mouth completely and grip its prey with no chance of escaping. The GREAT BARRACUDA is the biggest fish, reaching up to 2 metres in length. Unfortunately the larger fish – anything over 2.5kg – can carry the toxin ciguatera, though these fish are confined to the warmer waters of the western Atlantic, from Florida down to the Caribbean. The toxins, which appear to develop in the fish from eating a type of algae called benthic alga, have a 12 per cent fatality rate in unfortunate consumers as cooking

does not destroy them. Luckily the toxin doesn't appear in the most popular barracuda for eating, the PACIFIC BARRACUDA or YELLOWTAIL BARRACUDA. The similar STRIPED SEAPIKE from South-east Asia, the Pacific and Australia can carry the toxin, but this is rare.

Silver scabbard fish

I first came upon the SILVER SCABBARD FISH in the early 1980s in the fish market in Mapusa in Goa, India; I'd never seen anything like them before. Now they're common in specialist fish markets such as Billingsgate, in Britain. Back then though, they looked like strange creatures with their dusty, stainless-steel-like skin, long, flat sword-shaped bodies and frightening array of needle-sharp teeth. All scabbard fish are, in fact, very good eating, having firm, white meat that's coarse-textured but delicately flavoured, like eels. The tail sections are hard work to eat, being more bone than anything else, but sections of the body are good baked, grilled, pan-fried or used in soups and stews.

A similar species in the Atlantic, the BLACK SCABBARD FISH, is considered a great delicacy by the Portuguese and is caught off the island of Madeira at a depth of over 1,000 metres. Fishing for them is a wonder of skill and tradition: the long lines have to be dyed black with a dye made from the bark of a particular Madeiran tree. The fish are fearsome-looking – shiny and black with fierce teeth and vengeful eyes – which might explain why they are of little importance elsewhere. SOUTHERN FROSTFISH and RIBBON FISH are two other names for the same fish found in Australia and New Zealand, where they are caught as a by-catch of trawling for demersal (bottom-feeding) fish.

Garfish

The other main fish in this 'elongated' family is the Garfish, *Belone belone*. Very similar species occur in northern Europe

and Australia and New Zealand, though the European variety is perhaps more exotic due to its bones being of a bright green hue. These are said to make the fish less popular – I suppose people think they might be poisonous – but this is not so and their flesh is excellent, firm and fresh-tasting and slightly oily. It's not a fish that you're likely to get in fishmongers in the UK, but in Australia it's much more common and they are sold whole or as butterfly fillets – still joined along the back.

A similar fish, which is often considered one and the same, is the NEEDLEFISH, SAURY or SKIPPER, *Scomberesox saurus*, called BALAOU or AIGUILLE DE MER in French. Though this fish is most common in the Atlantic, west from Madeira right across to the Caribbean where it is eaten fried or grilled, it also swims as far north as Norway in the summer. It's popular in Denmark, fried and served with a sauce verte and boiled potatoes.

Lastly there's the BARRACOUTA, from Australia and New Zealand. With soft, light-tasting flesh it was widely used in the fish-and-chip trade there, but has largely been replaced by other fish such as flathead and flake (the common name for the GUMMY SHARK and SCHOOL SHARK).

FLATFISH

In the waters off Great Britain we have the greatest range of flatfish anywhere in the world and, unfortunately for the rest of the world, the two best flatfish, the DOVER SOLE and TURBOT, occur only on the eastern side of the Atlantic and the Mediterranean.

Flatfish are ideal for those who don't like bones – there are none in the fillets. All flatfish have delicate white flesh made from muscle used to long inactivity with occasional bursts of energy. Having observed the farming of both turbot and halibut I would say that they are ideally suited to aquaculture since most of their life is spent motionless on the sea bed, almost camouflaged under the sand.

They are waiting for food, which, when it swims nearby, is eaten with great alacrity.

All flatfish begin life as conventional round fish but, as they grow, the eyes migrate to either the left or right side of the fish, enabling them to see in all directions when on the sea bed. The top and bottom of a flatfish are therefore the two flanks, not the back and belly. Left-sided flatfish are called sinistral and right-sided fish dextral. Most flatfish are right-sided; the left-sided ones are TURBOT, BRILL, MEGRIM, SCALDFISH and TOPKNOT.

Nowhere in the naming of fish are the common names more confusing than with flatfish. The name of Dover for the most exquisite of soles has nothing to do with its habitation. Historically, Dover was where the fish for the London market were landed. Also, the name DOVER SOLE, *Solea solea*, can mean either the EUROPEAN SOLE or PACIFIC FLOUNDER, *Microstomus pacificus*. In fact this last is a deep-water flatfish which can reach up to 4.5kg, and, because it is especially slimy, is only marketed in fillet form. The alternative name of Dover sole – ENGLISH SOLE – doesn't help either, as this is also the name of a good quality flounder, *Parophrys vetulus*, found all the way from Northern Mexico to Alaska. TURBOT, *Rhombus maximus*, is similarly difficult. Its name in Europe (it's turbot in French too) is also the name for several species of Pacific Flounder.

Turbot
Turbot is possibly the best tasting fish in the world. It has the perfect combination of firm, thick fillets of moist white flesh. The texture is dense and slightly gelatinous which means that it remains juicy after cooking and is never dry tasting. It is particularly suited to cooking on the bone in steak or 'tronçon' form, cut from good, large fish, weighing from 3–8kg so that the pieces are nice and thick. This is one of the few fish I cook with confidence as the main course for a banquet.

I prefer this exquisite fish served up in a simple form, probably just grilled with hollandaise sauce and a slice of lemon. The price of turbot is now heading into the same bracket as lobster – deservedly so. However, I don't think turbot under 1kg in weight, often called CHICKEN TURBOT, is particularly interesting. The smallest size worth cooking whole would be about 2kg. One of the pleasures of eating whole turbot is the gelatinous, fatty flesh near to the side fins, which will have been removed if the fish is filleted.

Dover sole
Filleting is a fate that falls to far too many DOVER SOLES, which would be better left whole. There are surely no better pan-sized fish than Dover soles when skinned and fried whole à la meunière (dusted with seasoned flour) and finished with a little beurre noisette and lemon (see page 283). An ideal-sized flatfish for eating whole weighs between 300g and 500g. Larger Dover soles are cheaper than the single-portion-sized ones and produce excellent, firm white fillets. Dover soles are not at their best when eaten immediately after they have been caught as their natural firmness makes them too tough – they need one or two days after catching for the flavour and texture of the flesh to develop. I always think that eating a Dover sole is like eating a perfect steak. Everything about it is just simple uncomplicated pleasure, even down to the fact that the fillets are easy to lift off, as the skeleton stays intact after cooking. No wonder they are just as popular in New York as in London and Paris.

Plaice, flounder and dabs
PLAICE and FLOUNDER have a similar flavour to Dover sole but, unlike them, are best eaten as soon as possible after being caught, since the fresh 'ozone' flavour of both fish quickly dissipates. Although they can be served on the bone or in fillet form, I think plaice and flounder are only worth eating whole when no more than a couple of days old.

Otherwise they are best filleted, floured, egg-and-breadcrumbed and deep-fried. This cooking method nurtures the flavour of slightly dull fish. Small whole DABS are good cooked like this and served with tartare sauce.

The Danish have an appetizing way with whole plaice, flounder or dabs, which they call *Bakskuld*: they lightly brine the fish, then hot smoke them and fry them in butter. It's a speciality of Esbjerg in West Jutland, and excellent with ice-cold aquavit or beer.

In the USA the name FLOUNDER refers to a number of fish of rather better eating quality than our own flounder, all belonging to the Pleuronectidae family. The WINTER FLOUNDER (or BLACKBACK), considered to be the best tasting of the US flounder, has very sweet, fine-flaked, firm, white meat. Although on average they weigh 450–900g, the biggest can weigh about 3kg and are often called sea flounders to distinguish them from the smaller bay fish. The SUMMER FLOUNDER, or FLUKE, also has an excellent flavour and is usually sold weighing between 500g and 2.5kg, but can reach up to 9 or 10kg.

Lemon sole
British LEMON SOLE has a longer-lasting flavour than the local flounders, plaice and dabs and is thus a better bet for grilling whole if you buy your fish from the average supermarket fish counter. Other good pan-sized flatfish are MEGRIM SOLE (or WHIFF) and WITCH SOLES or TORBAY SOLES, both of which are rather underrated and are therefore good value. The name 'lemon sole' in the US is a market name for another winter flounder and no more accurate a name than the British name for the fish lemon sole, which is not a true sole at all. It would be more accurate to call it a lemon dab.

Brill
Brill is similar in shape to turbot, though without the little hard nodules on the darker side. It tends not to be so big –

I've never seen one bigger than 5kg – and is more oval in shape. It too has a great flavour, although softer and less dense in texture than turbot. Like turbot though, the bigger the fish the better the eating. I tend to cook brill with slightly more complicated accompaniments than turbot because it is not quite as special. In Gilbert and Sullivan's operetta *HMS Pinafore* turbot is described as 'ambitious brill'.

Halibut
Halibut, though a lovely fish, is not quite as fine as turbot. It's the largest of all flatfish and the only one to occur on both sides of the Atlantic and, indeed, in a very similar form in the Pacific too. Whole fish can reach up to 100kg and are therefore always sold in fillet or steak form. It is a remarkably thick meaty fish, the cooking of which needs to be done with care to avoid dryness. An interesting fact about farmed halibut is that in the cold months the fish tend to go into limbo. Fish farmers have discovered that putting a few cod in the tanks encourages the halibut to start feeding earlier in the year. Presumably the cod that accompany halibut in the wild are harbingers of spring.

GROUPERS, SEA BASS AND BARRAMUNDI
To those of us living in Europe, groupers represent an exotic family of fish conjuring up an image of the southern states of the USA and the Pacific coast, the Caribbean and Australasia. The reason for this is that this fish does not occur in any significant numbers in European waters, except for the MEDITERRANEAN GROUPER (the MÉROU), known in the UK as the BLACK GROUPER.

Groupers have slightly squat, deep bodies and tend to be rather round and chunky-looking. They are generally excellent eating and the plus point is their versatility. You can barbecue them or bake them whole, but they also lend themselves to being filleted and served with delicate sauces. Try a simple sauce vierge – a warm olive oil dressing spiked with tomato, olives, anchovy and garlic – as with the turbot on page 234. These are customer-friendly fish – they look colourful and attractive, they've got plenty of flavour, and you don't need to be a trained chef to cook them with success.

You can now buy very well-flavoured groupers in London – and, with a little notice, probably from good quality fishmongers elsewhere. They come from all over the place and the tip, if you're thinking of what to do with a grouper, is to cook it in exactly the same way as you would a sea bass, to which they are closely related.

By far the biggest variety of groupers live in the USA, the largest of which is the ATLANTIC JEWFISH, which can reach weights of up to 300kg, but these are now seriously under threat from over-fishing. Groupers are most common around coral reefs and the rocky outcrops of the US continental shelf. While not so susceptible to trawling, they have suffered considerably from hook-and-line fishing, being large and therefore prized by amateur anglers. A further twist to their fate is that they are hermaphrodites, i.e. they all start life as females and become males as they grow larger. Overfishing has led to an acute shortage of males as these are the larger fish and therefore more attractive to anglers. The most popular are the RED GROUPER, SPOTTED CABRILLA and the YELLOWMOUTH GROUPER. The red grouper can weigh up to 25kg but the average weight on sale is between 2kg and 7kg. But unless you want to feed eight or more people, the most convenient way of buying it is in steak or fillet form. The meat is firm, white and sweet and is comparable with the far more expensive snapper. A great advantage of the flesh is that it is free from intermuscular bones but the skin tends to be tough and strongly flavoured so it is usually removed before cooking. The flesh is also often cubed and deep-fried in batter or used in the fish chowders of the southern states (see page 104).

The BLACK SEA BASS, closely related to the grouper, is a very popular fish in the USA and is especially favoured by the Chinese and Italians. It has firm white meat with a delicate flavour – probably produced by its mainly crustacean diet – and can be cooked using most methods.

In Australia there is a much smaller family of groupers that inhabits the tropical and subtropical waters, and these are generally called ROCK CODS. The most common members are the CORAL COD, COMMON CORAL TROUT, ESTUARY ROCK COD and BLACKTIP ROCK COD, this last being considered one of Australia's best eating fish with a distinctively flavoured, firm white flesh. But all of them are good eating, with wide and thick fillets.

Sea bass
The EUROPEAN SEA BASS is the most sought-after perch species for cooking. A very attractive fish, it has beautiful silvery skin but evil spines, which can cause very painful wounds. It has a dense, slightly soft-textured flesh and a very delicate, superior flavour. It's now farmed widely, though most farmed bass are still too small to be at their best. A good-sized fish is 1.5kg. If sold intact, remove the guts as soon as possible as the stomach is prone to bursting and this will taint the delicate flesh.

The WRECKFISH (also known as STONE BASS) appears in Cornwall in the summer months. Apparently at that time of year the fish follows floating flotsam towards the north from warmer, more southerly waters. It appears on both sides of the Atlantic but it is a case of feast or famine: you might get two weeks of nothing but wreckfish, and then not see another one for three years. Its flavour is similar to other bass and I've always found it very good value. The same fish in Australia and New Zealand, HAPUKA or HAPUKU, is among the most highly priced fish there. What could be a better example of the global nature of so many species of fish?

One of the most prized fish in the USA is the STRIPED BASS (also called ROCKFISH). I once caught a 12kg striped bass in Chesapeake Bay, which left me astonished as to how big this excellent fish grows – and apparently it was not a particularly big one. This is a story of the successful conservation of a fish, the angling for which is far more profitable to the local community than the previous commercial fishery, which hounded the striped bass close to extinction. Like all perches, this is not a particularly oily fish, falling somewhere between cod and salmon, and it's therefore very versatile since it can be cooked in the same way as either.

Barramundi
In Australia, the BARRAMUNDI (also called GIANT SEA PERCH) has an idiosyncratic shape, with a head that is disproportionately large in relation to its deep body. As with sea bass, it is now widely farmed but disappointing because of the small size at which the fish are sold. A good-sized fish is 2kg. The wild fish are very well flavoured, with thick soft fillets, which are good cooked in any way. Although a marine species, it is also found in the freshwater creeks and rivers of northern Australia where, presumably, it goes to spawn.

HERRING FAMILY
Herring
The maritime countries of northern Europe have made use of the HERRING in as many diverse culinary ways as the rural people of France have used the pig. Just think of the different ways herring is served up: kippers, bloaters, buckling, red herrings, roll mops, Bismarck herrings, pickled herrings, matjes herrings.

It's a shame, though, that our taste for oily fish such as herring seems to have disappeared because, fresh out of the sea, there's probably no better tasting fish. It is also becoming increasingly clear that the old adage 'Fish is good for you' is true. The herring is an oily fish rich in omega-3 polyunsaturated fatty acids, which appear to lower the risk of heart disease. Many people think the increase in heart disease is due to a decrease in oily fish consumption and point out that the Japanese, great fish eaters, have a far lower rate of heart disease than people in the West. It's also believed that omega-3 is essential for the development of a foetus in the womb.

Though the same species of herring stretches right across the North Atlantic, there are subtle regional differences. NORWEGIAN or ICELANDIC HERRING are those favoured by fish smokers as the larger fish, which weigh about 225g, look more impressive, and the greater fat content and bulk leads to a moister product. The BALTIC HERRING is smaller, on average about 150g, than the Atlantic herring, as are the herrings from the North Sea. Wet-cured herrings from the Baltic, however, made from smaller, leaner fish, have a distinctive flavour.

There is also an important herring fishery on the Pacific coast of North America where the fish can weigh up to 700g, though the average is about 300g. This is the main source of our herring milt, for which there's a recipe on page 213.

One of the problems with cooking all oily fish is the smell. When perfectly fresh the smell is very appetizing, but there's no denying that as the fish goes stale the smell is quite off-putting. Assuming you've bought the freshest herrings, I think that grilling them whole is preferable to any other way. But I also like them filleted (it's the bones that so many people find objectionable in herrings), dusted with medium-coarse oatmeal and pan-fried with a little oil and butter and a rasher of bacon.

I found this account of a Lowestoft drift-trawler crew's breakfast – at which the average consumption was nine herrings per person – in an old book called *The Fish Retailer and his Trade* by William Wood, published in 1933. 'There is tea, bread and butter in plenty and a wolfish appetite. The herrings have been taken straight from the net and gutted, beheaded and the tails cut off, then they have been slashed across the back with a large jack knife and this slashing seems to hold the secret of the success of this cooking because it allows the boiling fat, into which the herring is plunged, to get a real hold of the flesh. When the cooking is finished, in a few minutes, there is a huge tin dishful of the herrings, crisped and browned and with a flavour that is never approached on shore.'

Cured herrings
These products are more important economically than the fresh fish to the herring-fishing countries.

BISMARCK HERRINGS are filleted, unskinned herrings, which are cured in vinegar, brine and sugar and packed with slices of onion.

BLOATERS are whole, ungutted (and therefore plump-looking) salted herrings, which are cold-smoked for just 12 hours, leaving them with a slightly gamey flavour.

BUCKLING are hot-smoked, headless salted herring and can be purchased either gutted or ungutted. This renders them ready-to-eat, like smoked trout, with bread and butter, lemon and horseradish cream.

HARENG SAUR are the French equivalent of kippers, gutted and salted aboard the boat then smoked at a factory close to the landing point.

KIPPERS are fat herring, split from head to tail and air-dried then cold-smoked.

MATJES HERRINGS or 'MAIDEN HERRING' are young herring, which have been skinned and hand-filleted, then mild cured in sugar, salt, vinegar and spices.

PICKLED HERRING is merely the term for gutted herring, which has been dry-salted in barrels.

RED HERRINGS, called GENDARME in French, are little used these days but are salted and long smoked whole herring, which turn a deep red colour after about three weeks. They were preserved for storing in tropical countries without refrigeration.

ROLLMOPS are Bismarck herring fillets rolled around a pickle or onion slices and secured with a wooden skewer.

Sardines and pilchards

Much of what I've said about herring applies to sardines, pilchards and sprats as well. SARDINES have a certain cachet, associated as they are with charcoal grills and robust local wine in the Mediterranean. PILCHARDS were devilishly difficult to sell in the UK, but renamed as 'Cornish sardines' (pilchards are, in fact, adult sardines), they have gone on to sell rather well.

Maybe it's the weather, but the market for sardines for barbecuing is gradually growing. Wouldn't it be nice if there were small beach cafés all along the British coast serving little more than local grilled fish? At Saint Jean-de-Luz near Biarritz, one of France's main sardine ports, there's a restaurant that specializes in only two dishes – grilled sardines or grilled tuna with local Basque wine. It's always packed. You get a salad, sardines and chips. What more could you ask for?

In my first TV series, I made a film of my son, Jack, barbecuing sardines on a beach near my house. I drank some red wine and made a tomato, red onion and basil salad to go with them. I still regard it as the epitome of what I like about eating fish.

Anchovies and sprats

It's extremely rare to get fresh ANCHOVIES in fishmongers; they're really all destined for processing. Like SPRATS, they're a bit too small for most people to bother with, and unlike whitebait (see page 338) they can't be eaten whole and are therefore a bit fiddly. There's a technique for eating small oily fish though, which is to nibble along the backbone, then more or less suck the fillets off the bones, almost like a horse nuzzling at oats.

Like all oily fish, anchovies spoil very quickly and should be iced immediately after they are caught. Indeed, the reason that the flesh around the gut cavities of herrings, sardines and anchovies is often disintegrating when you buy them is because the guts have started to ferment on board the trawlers. For perfect condition, the temperature of oily fish like these should never rise above the temperature of the sea. Sprats keep better in this respect than anchovies, herrings and sardines. If you're lucky enough to get fresh anchovies in good condition, cook them in the same way as you would sardines. There's a suggestion for a dish in Jane Grigson's *Fish Cookery* (1973) which strikes me as worth seeking out; it's from Ischia in the Bay of Naples. The anchovies are boned and baked in olive oil, flavoured with oregano, then lemon juice is squeezed over just before serving.

Shad

The SHAD is a similar fish to the herring but much larger and more bony. The wild fish in Europe tend to weigh about 1.25kg, but commonly reach 2.5kg in America. Each fillet has three lines of bones running down it and needs to be dealt with by an accomplished filleter. This can be the only explanation as to why the fish is not more popular than it is because its taste ranks with the best salmon. The best time to eat shad is in May when it appears in estuaries in Europe and North America, before going upriver to spawn, but you can buy farmed shad in the Garonne region in France. Cook it in any way that you like to eat salmon. If you're lucky enough to get hold of the great roe of the female shad – described by an excellent seafood cook, Mark Bittman, as 'the foie gras of the fish world' – it should be dusted in seasoned flour, gently sautéed and served still pink.

Though not considered great eating in the North, the TARPON is more esteemed in West Africa. A southern member of the herring family, it can reach up to 2 metres in length and is a great game fish. The roes are much esteemed across the Atlantic in Central America.

JACKS, POMPANOS AND TREVALLIES

Jacks

The meat of all jacks is dark since they are pelagic (surface swimmers), and travel long distances. Like many other large pelagic fish, such as tuna and swordfish, they should be bled after capture by cutting off or slashing the tail.

Jacks are not well represented in Europe, though a species of HORSE MACKEREL (also known as SCAD) occurs all around Britain, and is primarily used as lobster bait. They fetch low prices because of their exterior of bony platelets. However, with these platelets removed, they are rather good cooked à la meunière (see page 238). The Japanese salt the bones, grill them until crisp, and serve with lemon and daikon sprinkled with lemon.

A close relative, the BLUEFISH, swims in the Mediterranean, as well as the Atlantic. In fact, being a long-distance pelagic fish, it also appears in Australia, where it is called TAILOR. This is a great fighting fish and a voracious eater. Although it is very nutritious, tailor or bluefish does not have a good shelf-life and, like other members of this group, benefits from having the dark protein line along the fillet removed, since it's rather harsh tasting. Bluefish is a bit like bonito in flavour. Both have dark and coarse flesh and neither are as fine tasting as tuna. Like bonito, too, it is much better undercooked and suits strong accompaniments such as garlic, soy, ginger and chilli.

With the exception of the POMPANO, jacks are not important commercially in America. This is because many of them are not particularly good eating and some of the larger tropical species occasionally suffer from ciguatera poisoning (see page 325). By far the best eating is the pompano, which is normally sold as a whole fish weighing between 750g and 1.5kg or as skin-on fillets. Its flesh is white but oily, meaty and sweet with an exquisite flavour. I think it's best grilled, though I once had it braised with tomato, garlic, fish stock and epazote – a rather pungent herb – in Vera Cruz in Mexico, which was startlingly good.

Nevertheless, the AMBERJACK is quite common in the southern states and, when smoked, is quite a delicacy in Florida. Mention too should be made of the CREVALLE JACK, a member of the *Caranx* genus, which is found in all tropical and subtropical seas in the world and is known in Australian waters as a TREVALLY.

Trevally

The fillet of this fish family is dark and the darker meat running along the centre of the fillet, under the skin, is best removed as it is quite overpowering. There are quite a number of species of trevallys in Indo-Pacific waters; the best tasting for me are the BLACK POMFRET and the YELLOWTAIL KINGFISH.

Cobia

The COBIA, also known as the BLACK KINGFISH, is not truly a jack, but in a family all on its own. It is a prime game fish which is also fished for commercially and is very fine tasting. It has a very tough skin so it is usually sold in fillet form and is also often sold smoked.

Dolphinfish

In a class of its own, is the MAHI MAHI, also called the DOLPHINFISH or DORADO. It's very popular in the Mediterranean, where it is known as LAMPUKI in Malta and LAMPUGA in Spain. It is very popular on both the Pacific and Atlantic coasts of the USA too. Like all the better quality members of this group, mahi mahi is excellent served raw as sashimi (see page 124).

MACKEREL AND TUNA

Like the jacks and trevallies above, mackerel and tuna are pelagic, long-roaming fish, which have dark oily

meat as a result. All species of mackerel and tuna are popular and widely fished commercially, so rather than describe each species, I have grouped them into three broad categories for cooking and eating purposes.

Small mackerel

All these small mackerels – the ATLANTIC MACKEREL, CHUB MACKEREL from the Mediterranean and the BLUE MACKEREL from Australian and New Zealand waters – average at less then 500g in weight, and are the fish of summer holidays all over the world. As with herrings, mackerel have to be jumping fresh. I prefer them grilled or pan-fried. Small mackerel can be cured in many of the ways that herring can – salted or smoked. Try preserving them as gravlax, page 193, to produce the Swedish gravad mackerel. They are also very good used in an escabeche (see page 216).

Large mackerel

The next group comprises all the mackerel ranging between 1kg and 5kg. These are the CERO, CHUB MACKEREL, KING MACKEREL (also called KINGFISH), SPANISH MACKEREL, WAHOO, FRIGATE MACKEREL, KAWAKAWA, SPOTTED MACKEREL and the BONITO. These again are all good eating, but the flesh tends to be coarser than that of the tunas and doesn't keep as well. While they can be successfully grilled, I think they are particularly good poached in oil, tandooried, or used in curries.

Large tuna

These are the BLUEFIN TUNA, YELLOWFIN TUNA and SKIPJACK TUNA, which fetch high prices for the Japanese sashimi market. They are available in all fish shops as dark red, meaty loins, or steaks that are good for searing and chargrilling as in the recipe on page 225. The ALBACORE, also called LONG-FIN TUNA, is in this category too but its meat is much

lighter in colour, and often called the 'chicken of the sea' or WHITE TUNA. It is to my mind a revelation when cooked on a good barbecue and, unlike Bluefin Tuna, is not in danger of being over-fished.

Tuna belly, which is rich in fat, is much esteemed by the Japanese. In sashimi (their elegant presentation of sliced raw fish) or sushi (vinegared rice topped with raw fish) it provides a flavourful contrast to the leaner loin meat. Being an oily fish it also lends itself to various types of curing. It is occasionally smoked, though I don't think this works very well. But, when cured and dried, then very thinly sliced, it makes a great addition to crunchy salads made with vegetables such as fennel and chicory. The Spanish blocks of dried tuna, called MOJAMA, are excellent.

MONKFISH AND STARGAZERS

Monkfish is in a group of its own – there is no other fish quite like it. Although there is a very similar species called GOOSEFISH or monkfish in America and another, STARGAZER or monkfish, in Australia and New Zealand, it's in Europe that the fish is really popular. I'm surprised it hasn't taken off elsewhere because it satisfies a universal desire for firm, meaty, boneless fish. Its flavour is not pronounced, though the small tails have a sweet freshness which, combined with the texture, make it one of my favourite fish. It's particularly suited to chargrilling and is also great in curries because it remains intact after cooking.

Once the fish is skinned, you'll find the fillets are encased in a thin membrane. You need to remove this or it will cause the tails to distort during cooking (see page 25).

WEEVER is an underrated fish in all parts of the world except for the Mediterranean. Weever has an excellent flavour and firm texture, almost on a par with Dover sole. Maybe its lack of popularity is due to the poisonous spines on the gill covers and the first spine on the dorsal fin, which can give you a sting that's a great deal worse than that of a bee. The pain lasts for about 12 hours, which accounts for the saying 'it's the following tide that takes the pain away'.

MULLETS
Red mullet
There's really no similarity between red and grey mullet except for the name and the fact that they can be cooked in much the same way. Both fish appear all over the world.

My favourite is the RED MULLET, particularly those species from the Mediterranean. All fish that live on a diet of crustaceans have a flavour somewhat echoing that of shellfish, but none more so than the red mullet. It has a perfect flake and skin which, when grilled, smells of rock pools. If you are lucky enough to get an ungutted red mullet, the liver is something of a delicacy too. Indeed the first red mullet I ever ate was grilled with its liver intact and in this form is known as *bécasse de mer*. *Bécasse* is French for woodcock and, like the woodcock, it doesn't have a gall bladder, so provided that the intestine is removed, the rest will not taste bitter.

The red mullet has the same name in Australia but is often called GOATFISH there, which is also the most common name for a very similar species of mullet in America. There are five different species on both the Atlantic and Pacific coasts, but they are most commonly found in Florida and the Caribbean.

Grey mullet
The GREY MULLET is generally less regarded around the world. Unfortunately, they have an erroneous reputation for feeding on sewage. The mullet in the bays around Padstow, which sometimes have a golden flash on the gill cover, are just as good to eat as bass.

The grey mullet is either called grey mullet or STRIPED MULLET in the USA. The *Encyclopedia of Fish Cookery* by A. J. McClane is an excellent book and one I've referred to a lot in writing this section. In it the author describes an attempt in Florida to increase grey mullet sales as follows: 'The State of Florida chose the seemingly romantic name "Lisa" to promote sales of the fish. This was no more comprehensible than a plague of bullfrogs. The consumer invariably asked, "What is a Lisa?" and when the retailer explained that it was a mullet, nothing was accomplished, except to suggest that the fish had to be disguised.'

Grey mullet is known as MULLET, SEA MULLET, or DIAMOND-SCALE MULLET in Australia and New Zealand.

PUFFER FISH
I must confess that I have never eaten PUFFER FISH but I'd certainly like to. Apparently it's one of the most delicate fish in the sea, the creamy white meat being similar to a plump frog's leg. Puffers, which are known as SEA SQUABS or BLOWFISH in America, are found from Cape Cod down to Florida, but the largest number of species (thirty-eight) are found around Japan and it is from here that the fame of the world's most poisonous fish stems. It seems that the more fatalities are caused by pufferfish, or FUGU as it is known, the more popular it becomes. There are on average seventy deaths a year, usually in rural areas where people prepare the fish at home. The poison, found in the gut, liver, ovaries and skin of the fish, is called tetrotoxin. It's similar to curare (the poison used by the Amazonian Indians to tip their arrows), and is 1,250 times deadlier than cyanide.

Kitaoji Rosanjin, the famous Japanese potter and gourmet wrote: 'The taste of fugu is incomparable; if you eat it three or four times you are enslaved; anyone who declines it for fear of death is a really pitiable person.' A chef must be licensed to prepare fugu and this requires a written and practical examination that includes eating the fugu he has prepared. Prior to that the chef must have completed at least two years working under a master. Death by fugu poisoning is described as terrible: although you can think clearly, you cannot speak or move, and soon cannot breathe. But enthusiasts say consumption of the meat produces a pleasant, warm tingling, a faint echo of the poison. Perhaps eating unprepared fugu is one of the favoured ways of committing hara-kiri (suicide). As the haiku poet Yosa Buson wrote:
> 'I cannot see her tonight.
> I have to give her up
> So I will eat fugu'

ROE FISH
Here I've included fish that are most important for their roe (eggs). Some fish, such as LUMPFISH, are only valuable for their roe – which is similar to caviar in appearance, but not in taste – while other fish, such as STURGEON, have tasty flesh as well as roe. Sturgeon has very firm flesh with a high oil content. It is sold in North America as steaks or is preserved in wine vinegar and spices, but it is most often sold smoked.

It is the roe of the BELUGA, OSCIETRA and SEVRUGA STURGEON that forms the world's most luxurious food – CAVIAR. Caviar from farmed sturgeon is produced near Bordeaux in France, and California in America. The flavour of caviar grows on you: the first time most people taste it it's a little disappointing, but there's something about the salty, oiliness of it that makes you give it a second try and then – like some fiendish drug – it becomes an expensive obsession. Sevruga is the cheapest caviar and beluga the most expensive, mainly because it comes from the largest of the sturgeons and the eggs are therefore bigger. I think oscietra is the perfect compromise.

To make caviar, the master caviar-maker removes the sac of roe from the fish and then rubs it through a fine screen, allowing the eggs to pass through whole but removing blood and membrane. The roe is then rinsed and salted. Adding the right amount of salt – between 3 and 5 per cent – is where the caviar-maker's art lies. The freshest roe requires the least salt and good caviar will always have the label 'molossol' or 'malossol', which means 'little salt'.

Here are a few tips on how best to enjoy caviar:
• Avoid pasteurized caviar. Only buy fresh and allow about 25g per person.
• As long as it hasn't been opened, caviar will keep for 6–9 months in the coldest part of the fridge, but the sooner it's eaten the better.
• Remove the caviar from the fridge half an hour before serving. Nestle the tin in some crushed ice and use a non-metal spoon to serve it – mother of pearl or even plastic are good – as caviar reacts with metal.
• Serve simply with thin wholemeal toast, blinis or good fresh bread. Some classic accompaniments are blinis brushed with melted butter, or topped with sour cream or crème fraiche. In addition, Russians serve caviar accompanied by finely chopped onions and chopped hard-boiled eggs, both of which are said to bring out the flavour of the fish eggs.

Other roe
The roes of some other fish are worthy of note. Both the eggs and the MILT of herring are delicious. The Japanese lightly salt the roe of the female and use it in sashimi, while the milt, the white seminal fluid of the male, is excellent floured and shallow-fried (see page 213). It's a good idea to disgorge the milt for ten minutes or so in water, to which lots of lemon juice has been added, before drying and coating it for cooking. I've recently been using lightly smoked herring roe with a lot of success, adding half a teaspoon of it to a cream sauce and serving it with salmon escalopes. I've also mentioned shad roe, sometimes called the 'foie gras of the sea', under the entry for the herring family (see page 329).

If you can get hold of the Greek salted and dried GREY MULLET ROE (BOTARGO), it is nice sliced into very thin strips and served with olive oil, pepper and lemon juice as a very pleasant mezze, or added like anchovies to salads to give them piquancy. SMOKED SALTED COD ROE is now a common substitute for grey mullet roe in the making of the Greek dish taramasalata. Lightly salted salmon eggs called KETA are something of a delicacy (see the recipe for Nigiri Sushi on page 123).

SALMON AND SEA TROUT
There are six species of SALMON native to the northern hemisphere. There are none in the southern hemisphere, although you wouldn't realize it because the farming of salmon in Tasmania means that ATLANTIC SALMON is just as common there. Atlantic salmon is the fish that is always used for farming. Like it or not, farmed salmon has encouraged more people to eat fish as it is now cheap and readily available. It's got lots of flavour and suits cooking in almost any way, though not in batter; it's too oily a fish for that.

There's a great deal of controversy about the farming of salmon because, when done unscrupulously, it can have a devastating effect on the wild stocks of other fish as well as salmon, due to the build up of parasites, disease and chemicals in an overpopulated environment. Some would like to see all salmon farms banned. But when the fish are kept further out at sea, rather than in the more usual lochs and estuaries, or where the fish densities are kept at a sensible level and the fish are well looked after, far less damage is caused. It is worth paying the price for premium quality farmed salmon, particularly if it is organically farmed. It tastes so much better; the flesh is firmer and not overwhelmingly fatty and you are less likely to be damaging the environment.

My favourite way to cook salmon and sea trout is to poach them whole in salted

water and serve them with homemade mayonnaise (see page 311), new potatoes and a cucumber and mint salad. I'm also particularly fond of seasoning a steak or two of salmon and cooking them gently in butter in a frying pan. I add half a glass of white wine halfway through cooking and let the liquid reduce, then finish the dish off with some chopped parsley.

Atlantic salmon
WILD ATLANTIC SALMON is still my favourite but there is a severe shortage, mostly through over-fishing rather than any disasters caused by farming. I mourn the decline of the wild Atlantic salmon and get depressed when I hear that the Rhine was once teeming with them. We're lucky that we can still buy some wild salmon from the estuary on which our restaurant stands; the lean taste of the wild fish, which has swum so far, is incomparable. Atlantic salmon was also found on the east coast of Canada and North America but it has suffered a decline similar to that of the same species in Europe.

Pacific salmon
There are six other salmon, all from the Pacific coast, which are in much better shape. The biggest of them all is the CHINOOK SALMON, also called the KING SALMON, sometimes reaching as much as 50kg. It's a large-flaked fish with a high fat content and soft texture. Next, there's the COHO SALMON, which is smaller – it reaches 15kg – and the fillet is lighter in colour than the chinook. The SOCKEYE SALMON's name has nothing to do with the eyes but is a corruption of an Indian word. Both the male and female sockeye salmon become bright red on spawning. They have very dark, almost orange flesh, with a firm texture and delicate taste. The CHUM SALMON, which weighs up to 15kg, is, along with pink salmon, cheaper than the others and somewhat coarse in texture. It probably fetches a lower price because its flesh colour is often more grey than pink, but it takes to smoking well. The PINK SALMON is the smallest Pacific

salmon, never weighing more than 5kg. It is the cheapest salmon of all except the chum, but has a delicate, distinctive flavour and a good pink colour.

Sea trout

I'm almost more fond of WILD SEA TROUT than I am of Atlantic salmon. The small ones we get at the restaurant, fresh from the sea during the months of May and June, are one of the great pleasures of early summer, as are the spider crabs that arrive on the rocky beaches just below the low-tide mark (at exactly the same time as the thrift blooms in the stone walls and hedges in the fields above).

A sea trout, also known as SALMON TROUT, SEWIN or OCEAN TROUT, is a freshwater brown trout that has gone to sea. Why some members of the same species should travel down rivers, through the brackish waters of estuaries into the sea to feed on prawns and other crustaceans – which produce the characteristic pink colour of the flesh – is unclear. But something in their genetic make-up enables them to develop a silvery sheen and the ability to cope with the osmotic effect of salt in the water. They don't follow the same migratory pattern as salmon but stay in relatively near-coastal waters before returning up-river to spawn. Predictably they have a taste somewhere between trout and salmon, being less rich than salmon and slightly less pink. Incidentally, large sea trout and small salmon look very similar. The only sure way to tell the difference is to look at the eyes: those of a sea trout are slightly higher up the head. If you draw an imaginary line from the mouth through to the centre of the gill cover it will bisect the eye of a salmon, but a salmon trout's eye will be above it.

Char and smelt

There are a couple of other members of the salmon family that are worthy of note. There are two types of CHAR or ARCTIC CHAR: those that live most of their lives in their sea and swim up northern rivers to spawn, and landlocked char, which can be found in many lakes all over northern Europe (including Lake Windermere in England), Canada and Alaska. The sea-going variety makes by far the best eating and reaches up to 13kg in size. It is a fat fish, with firm red flesh when caught in the wild, but less firm or deeply coloured when farmed.

The SMELT (also called RAINBOW SMELT or SPARLING), a small member of the salmon family reaching no more than 28cm in length, is found in both Northern Europe and North America. The fish have a characteristic smell of cucumbers when very fresh and generally have light green skin, soft flesh and bones. They deteriorate incredibly rapidly and like so many oily fish – herrings, mackerel, sardines – should be cooked the day they're caught. However, as long as they're chilled straight after catching and frozen soon after, then defrosted to a temperature of no more than 1°C and cooked from that temperature, they will be almost as good as fresh ones. The best way to cook the smaller ones is to thread them on to wooden skewers and grill or fry them in clarified butter where, because of their soft open texture, they'll take no more than 2–3 minutes. They are also particularly nice whole, coated in tempura batter and deep-fried.

Smoked salmon

All members of the salmon family can be smoked successfully but none more so than salmon itself. Cold-smoked salmon, where the fish is subjected to smoke without heat, is now so popular that its luxury status has all but disappeared and much of the cheap, pre-sliced stuff you can buy is just pink, flabby and boring. However, a side of salmon, not necessarily wild, but with a good high fat content, cured maybe with salt and brown sugar and smoked over oak chippings, beech or whisky barrels for at least 8 hours, is still something very special. Hot-smoked salmon called BRADAN ROST is good served on lightly griddled slices of sourdough bread with mixed, small salad leaves and a chive, caper and crème fraîche dressing.

SEA BREAM, PORGIES AND SNAPPERS

This section looks just at SEA BREAM, not freshwater bream. There are many species, but all bream are firm-fleshed fish with medium oil content, although smaller ones tend to be a bit bony. They are well flavoured, thanks to a diet of crustaceans, and have a pleasing, compact body shape, which makes them ideal for steaming, grilling or cooking on a barbecue. One of the unifying features of all bream is that they generally come in one- or two-portion sizes i.e. 500g–1kg. However, there are plenty of exceptions. I've seen snappers as big as 4kg. Once, while on holiday in Cephalonia, six of us dined on a sumptuous *synagrida* (the Greek word for the DENTEX), served with Greek salad and chips fried in olive oil, and washed down with copious quantities of Robola, a very good local white wine.

Red bream

In Padstow in the 1970s and '80s, we used to have regular landings of RED BREAM caught very close to the coast near Newquay. They are firm textured and sweet with a thick skin and amazingly large scales. Their subtle red colour and enormous eyes also make them one of the most attractive fish. I used to serve them baked on a bed of haricot beans with chilli, bay leaf, garlic, olive oil, orange juice and zest. I recall having a boy working in the kitchen for the summer holiday once. When I asked him to gut the fish he cut off all their heads which, owing to the round shape of a bream and his inexperience, meant that half the fillet went with it too. He's now a successful surgeon, I'm still a chef, and every time I see him he recalls with acute embarrassment the beheading of the red bream. I wish I could go back to those days because there are no red bream left and they were one of my favourite fish.

In fact, all the bream and the closely related PORGY from America are good eating, but the red bream and the most highly esteemed GILTHEAD BREAM (*daurade* in French) are the best in Europe. We buy a lot of local BLACK SEA BREAM, which is reasonably good eating. I like them steamed whole with garlic and ginger, as I've done for the recipe with grey mullet on page 151. And although the scales on bream are always plate-like, once they're removed the skin is often soft and pleasing to eat, particularly when steamed in this way. In America, the most highly regarded porgies are the SHEEPSHEAD BREAM and the SCUP which, when whole, weigh from 350g to 1.5kg, and have flaky, tender and very tasty flesh. Interestingly, the EUROPEAN SEA BREAM and the AMERICAN RED PORGY appear to be one and the same fish. As a result of a relatively comprehensive study of the migration of these fish, it is clear that fish appear in different far-flung parts of the world, not generally through a migratory habit, but rather through the eggs drifting on the ocean currents.

How else might we explain the presence in Australian and New Zealand waters of the same group of fish, the Sparidae? The best-flavoured examples of these are the BLACK BREAM, the YELLOWFIN BREAM, the SWEETLIP BREAM, the FRYPAN BREAM and the SNAPPER. In fact, this snapper, which is one of Australia's most highly regarded fish, is not a true snapper but a bream. Then again, there is another group of fish in Australasia called THREADFIN BREAM, which are not true bream. How confusing!

There is a small group of fish called bream that are actually more closely related to pomfret (see Thin-Bodied fish, page 339). These are the wide-ranging RAY'S BREAM, the *Brama brama*, which appear in the southern oceans off New Zealand and yet have also been landed on the beaches of Sussex.

Snappers
Snappers are a very important fish family and provide one of the best-tasting fish the sea has to offer, with their succulent, fantastically flavoured white meat. Owing to the wonders of airfreight we can now buy them here, almost as fresh and lively as fish from the quayside, though I have this rather depressed feeling that the quality could sometimes be better on a lot of supermarket counters. One of my favourites is the RED EMPEROR, also known as BOURGEOIS, EMPEROR or SNAPPER from Australia, and this is possibly the best fish I know for barbecuing. I've had great success chargrilling large fillets of red emperor. I make a marinade of olive oil, lemon zest, bay leaves, thyme, chilli flakes and salt, then I grill the fish, brushing it constantly with the same marinade.

A closely related species, from the Indian Ocean and Australia, which is also easy to get in the UK is the SPANGLED EMPEROR, known as CAPITAINE or BLUE EMPEROR. I cooked this once at a barbecue on Mauritius and served it with the mango, prawn and chilli salsa on page 176. Unfortunately, it happened to coincide with the only tropical rainstorm of the two-week trip.

In America the most sought-after fish in this family is the RED SNAPPER; others with good eating qualities are the MUTTON SNAPPER and YELLOWTAIL SNAPPER. But it's the red snapper that's the snapper for me. If you want fillets, the ideal weight to buy would be between 3.5kg and 5.5kg, but whole fish weighing between 500g and 1.5kg are also great for cooking whole.

Grunters
The first thing you'd want to know about a fish called a GRUNTER is – why? Well, it's because when they're caught they grind their teeth in panic and the sound is then amplified by their air bladder to make a grunt-like noise. The fish are related to snappers; they have a delicate white flesh but with a slightly softer texture and finer white flake. They tend to be small fish, no more than 500g in

size, and are ideal for cooking whole on a barbecue. Particularly good is the PORKFISH.

SEA CATFISH
Closely related to the freshwater catfish of the Mississippi, the Danube and other large rivers of Eastern Europe, SEA CATFISH, *Galeichthys felis*, has well-flavoured white, medium-firm flesh, which keeps well. The skins of all catfish are thick, slippery and strong like that of an eel and they therefore have to be skinned in the same way, but it is unusual to buy it in any form other than fillets.

The name catfish is also given to an unrelated species in northern Europe called the WOLF FISH, *Anarhichas lupus*, which is also called SEACAT, OCEAN CATFISH or ROCK TURBOT, and is of excellent quality. It has particularly firm white fillets and the first time I ate it I thought it tasted a bit like Dover sole, but it deteriorates much more quickly.

In America, by far the most popular way of cooking catfish is to coat it in cornmeal, often flavoured with things such as curry powder, chilli and even five-spice powder, and to fry it until crisp and golden. It is traditionally served with hush puppies (onion-flavoured cornmeal fritters) and lemon wedges. Interestingly, though the name catfish refers to the 'whiskers' or barbels situated near the mouth, the most striking feature of the American GAFFTOPSAIL CATFISH is the enormous Arabic dhow-sail-like dorsal fin. The similar species in Australia and New Zealand, CATFISH and COBBLER, though just as good in quality, are not as well appreciated as the American and European fish. However, there is a growing market in Western Australia for cobbler fillets, also known, inevitably, as catfish fillets.

SEA CREATURES
Most of the species in this section are pretty esoteric, and not even known to many people, but they have their

enthusiasts. Get talking to a Galician about percebes, or a Chinese about sea slugs, and you'd think you were talking about a delicacy waiting to take the world by storm. But I think the seafood lover should be familiar with all of these and most of the time they are very good to eat.

Percebes or gooseneck barnacles

The Galicians of northern Spain are mad about these strange brown barnacles, which are correctly classified as crustaceans. They look a bit like the legs of a tortoise, a bit shorter and stumpier than your little finger. They taste something like the claw meat of lobster and are boiled in salted water and eaten plain, often with Albariño, the local wine of Galicia. Percebes fetch big money in Spain because the fishing of them is dangerous. The fishermen, called *mariscadores*, prise them off the rocks at low tide and often risk being swept away.

Jellyfish

Although we don't eat JELLYFISH in the West, the Chinese dry the umbrella part of certain species. They are then rehydrated, cut into strips and served in a classic Chinese dish with strips of chicken, cucumber, coriander and soy. The jellyfish doesn't have much taste; it's more the texture that is valued. The edible species are *Rhopilema esculenta* and *Stomolophus nomurai* and, from Australian waters, *Aurelia aurita*, also known as the MOON JELLYFISH.

Sea urchin

The only edible part of a SEA URCHIN is the cluster of creamy or orange coloured roe, also known as corals. Though not common in fishmongers, urchins have many fans. They have a beautiful, fragrant flavour and are to be enjoyed spooned out of the opened and cleaned shell (see page 97) and eaten raw, folded into hot pasta (see page 273) or used to thicken a fine sauce. The best eating is the MEDITERRANEAN SEA

URCHIN, *Paracentrotus lividus*. This is the one with long black or dark brown spines. The urchin of Northern Europe and North America, the GREEN SEA URCHIN, has a much bigger 'test' (shell). In Orkney they are known as a 'Scarrimans Heid', meaning a street child with unruly spiky hair. This same urchin is present in the Northern Pacific as well, but there's a bigger species in Northern California, which reaches as much as 12.5cm in diameter. In Australia and New Zealand, the BLACK SEA URCHIN is more like the Mediterranean in shape but the roe is mostly exported to Asia.

Violets

This is a knobbly creature with leathery skin that lives anchored to rocks or the sea bed in the Mediterranean and is enjoyed in France and Italy. You cut them in half – the skin is violet in colour as you are cutting through it, hence the name. The inside, the bit you eat, is bright yellow. It's very soft, like scrambled egg, with a taste of ozone but quite bitter, as raw mussels can sometimes be. Shallot vinegar can offset this.

I've eaten the same sort of creature in New South Wales in Australia, but I haven't been able to track down the name of it in any book. Local fishermen put me on to them. They were nicer than Mediterranean violets, being less bitter.

Sea cucumbers

The Chinese hold SEA CUCUMBERS in great esteem. They look like fat slugs lying on the sea bed, about 25–35cm in length and weighing up to 2kg when alive. Once harvested, they are gutted, boiled and dried and sometimes smoked. They are then reconstituted in water before cooking. Sea cucumbers have strong longitudinal muscles and therefore need to be cut thinly crossways to make them edible. As with jellyfish, the Chinese enjoy their rubbery texture, liking a more comprehensive range of textures in their food than most of us do in the West.

SEA PERCH

This is a collection of similarly shaped fish with round, deep bodies, tough skins and large scales, and with the first and second dorsal fins joined, the first fin always being spiny. Their flesh is generally pinkish-white in colour, firm but open textured and therefore slightly flaky when cooked. Because of their medium oil content, they suit every type of cooking, particularly barbecues, hence the popularity of Surfperch in America and Dhufish in Australia at convivial al fresco meetings.

There are 20 types of SURFPERCH on the Pacific coast of America, ranging from Alaska down to the Baja California peninsula. These are not true perch but are similar in texture and for cooking purposes we can treat them the same. The best eating are the REDTAIL, the BARRED and the CALICO SURFPERCH. All are what you might call pan fish as they are never much bigger than 1–2kg, thus they can be pan-fried or cooked whole. The OPALEYE is also sold as perch, being very similar in size and shape. DRUMMERS are a group of fish in Australia which have a general perch-like appearance. One is the LUDERICK; the other best-known fish in this family is the SWEEP. These fish are essentially vegetarian and mainly feed on seaweed. Though they are good table fish, they can be tainted by iodine from the seaweed.

The DHUFISH, also known as JEWFISH, is one of the most sought-after Indian Ocean fish in Western Australia, so next time you're in Perth you'll know what to order at Fraser's fish restaurant overlooking the Swan River. Dhufish, and the closely related PEARL PERCH, which is available on the east coast, have excellent flavour and texture and are among the best fish on the continent.

SEA VEGETABLES
Carragheen (Irish moss)

A red or greenish-brown seaweed which grows in short, frilly tufts on coastlines of Europe and America. It is dried in the open air and bleaches to a creamy pink colour. It's traditionally used in Ireland to thicken milk puddings, and to make a vegetarian-friendly alternative to gelatine.

Dulse

An edible red seaweed that occurs in both the northern and southern hemispheres. It's most popular in Ireland where dried dulse is sold in the pubs of Belfast in little packets, as snacks.

Laver

Found around the coast of North America and Europe, laver is green when young, becoming purple, then dark brown as it ages. It is particularly popular in South Wales where, after harvesting, it is boiled to a purée. I think this goes extremely well with the cockles that would often have come from the same beach. Laver is also known as NORI in Japan and, in its dried form, pressed into thin sheets, it is used as the outer wrapping in nori sushi (see page 123).

Kelp

This name is given to several large varieties of brown seaweed which grow in the Atlantic and are used by local people in their traditional dishes.

Kombu

This name is given to a group of brown seaweeds, of which *Laminaria japonica* is the most common. When dried it is very important in Japanese cooking. Kombu and dried bonito flakes (katsuobushi) – a fish from the same family as tuna and mackerel – are the two ingredients needed for making dashi, the classic Japanese stock, which is used in many dishes. Kombu, which is very similar to the kelps that grow in the Atlantic, is very rich in monosodium glutamate.

Wakame

By far and away the most popular seaweed in Japan, wakame is a green, frilly-fronded seaweed, which is easy to buy dried and can be used in salads (see Crab with Wakame Salad on page 295) or cooked in soups.

Sea lettuce

The most widely distributed of edible seaweeds in the world, this is used in salads and soups.

Sea kale

This member of the cabbage family, which normally grows wild on the pebbly beaches of Europe, is bitter and inedible unless it has grown under sand. These days the young shoots of the new season's sea kale are covered and forced like rhubarb to present an early spring delicacy, which is excellent boiled and served like asparagus, with hollandaise sauce.

Marsh samphire

As its name suggests, this grows in muddy estuaries and tidal salt marshes around Europe. It's easy to identify, having unusual, light green branches rather than leaves and growing little more than 20cm off the mud. It is harvested in Britain between May and September, though earlier in more southern countries. Contrary to what many think, picking the whole plant out of the mud will not endanger stocks, as the plants grow from seed and not from regeneration of the roots. It has a delicious salty fresh taste, making it an ideal vegetable for serving with fish, and is particularly delicious when served with hollandaise sauce. It should be boiled – without salt in the water – until only just tender.

Rock samphire

Gatherers of this variety of samphire are described in *King Lear* as plying a 'dangerous trade', presumably referring to the need to scramble over the face of high cliffs to collect it. In my part of the world, it grows conveniently out of Cornish stone walls and low rocks by the beach. It has a pungent, aromatic smell, slightly reminiscent of fennel, and in fact belongs to the same family,

the Umbelliferae. Traditionally it was always pickled. I have had some success in using it as a herb for flavouring a cream sauce, but you have to be very parsimonious with it. To me it is the most evocative of plants, recalling childhood summer holidays strolling down sandy Cornish lanes.

SHARKS AND RAYS

Here I've grouped all those shark and shark-like fish that have cartilage rather than bones. There are a few other fish with cartilage rather than bone – notably the sturgeon and the lamprey – but these are not related to sharks and rays.

Sharks

The great plus of all sharks is that there are no bones in the flesh. All have lots of flavour, many with a slight tartness, particularly the Atlantic sharks – the PORBEAGLE and MAKO – which are excellent eating, though they are to be avoided in Europe due to overfishing.

Part of the assertive flavour of shark comes from the presence of urea in their flesh. All fish are less salty than the sea around them so, to avoid dehydration, they have to counteract osmosis (the tendency of salt to attract water). Sharks do this by producing urea, which is perfectly acceptable in fresh fish; however, after death urea gradually breaks down into ammonia and becomes repulsive in stale fillets. The advantage of this breakdown is that while quite a few sharks – notably skates and rays – are inedible when just caught, being incredibly tough, the subsequent break-up of the urea tenderizes the fish.

The BLACKTIP SHARK from Florida and the Caribbean has very white meat, a bit drier than MAKO and TIGER SHARK but in America most shark gets marketed as mako and sometimes mako gets marketed as swordfish, since the fillet is very similar. Other fine-tasting sharks in the Atlantic are the HAMMERHEAD SHARK, which also swim in Indo-Pacific waters.

In Australia the most popular eating sharks are the GUMMY SHARK, the WHISKERY SHARK and SCHOOL SHARK. The school and gummy sharks are sold in fish-and-chip shops as FLAKE. Australia and New Zealand also have a number of dogfish, skates and rays very similar to our own. They also have the ANGEL SHARK as do we, but this is confusingly also called monkfish both there and here. It looks similar to monkfish but its flavour is more like that of skate or ray, and it has small wings like they do, but without the long fibrous strands of flesh.

Rays

The naming of SKATE and RAY is a little confusing. Alan Davidson, perhaps the world's greatest culinary ichthyologist, suggests that the old distinction should stand, whereby we call skates the bigger fish with long snouts, and rays the smaller fish with rounded heads. In Britain the best ray for eating is the THORNBACK RAY. The BLONDE RAY is also good.

All skates and rays in the UK are considered to be under threat by the Marine Conservation Society. Look at their Good Fish Guide for guidance on what not to buy.

Skate and ray are at their best about 2–5 days old: after that point, the smell of the ammonia becomes most unpleasant and no amount of cooking will remove it.

Dogfish

Dogfish are small relatives of the shark family. The best DOGFISH is the SPUR-DOG though the LESSER SPOTTED DOGFISH, also called the ROUGH HOUND, MURGY or MORGAY is good. The NURSEHOUND and SMOOTH HOUND are also perfectly enjoyable and are used for the fish-and-chip trade as rock salmon or rock eel. All dogfish are also good with Indian masalas. Other popular names for dogfish are HUSS and ROCK SALMON, or *saumonette* in French, probably due to the pinkish-white colour of the flesh.

SHELLFISH – BIVALVES AND UNIVALVES

Bivalves

These are the shellfish that live in two, hinged shells. Unlike fish, there is little difference in the taste of CLAMS, MUSSELS or OYSTERS around the world. Some experts swear that they can taste the water in which they grow. Because of their similarity in taste, I have grouped all the bivalves by size: small, medium, large.

Small bivalves

I use small clams for a first course, such as Clams with XO sauce (page 262), and I find generally that MUSSELS and COCKLES can be used in the same way. The CARPETSHELL CLAM, called *vongole* in Italian, and *palourde* in France, is the best one for Linguine alle Vongole, although I've made it with PIPIS in Australia and been well pleased with it.

Though I have a nostalgic affection for the small beach mussels from around Padstow, we find that the best mussels to use for all our dishes are rope-grown farmed ones. Suspended in midwater in estuaries rich in plankton, rope mussels grow very quickly and are not attacked by predators such as crabs and starfish living on the bottom. Because they are always covered with water they are constantly feeding and develop a thinner shell than mussels that live on the shore and have to withstand the attrition of waves. The thin shell ensures that they cook quickly and uniformly.

The technique of opening small clams for serving raw on ice is illustrated on page 89, but you can also steam them open carefully in a covered pan, if you prefer, with a splash of water or wine. The trick is to take them out as soon as the shells pop open, so don't try to do too many at once – just enough to cover the base of the pan. You can open cockles by pushing the knuckle end (the hinge of the cockle) against the knuckle of another one and twisting.

Medium bivalves

I wouldn't tend to use the American MEDIUM QUAHOGS, LITTLENECKS, STEAMERS or CHERRYSTONES on a *fruits de mer* or in a pasta dish. I think of them more as a delicacy to be served on their own. I love a bowl of steamers with just drawn butter and the cooking liquor.

Large bivalves

I prefer to stuff larger mussels, such as the NEW ZEALAND GREENLIP MUSSEL, with garlic breadcrumbs. And I find that the larger the clam, the more the resistance to eating it whole. I persist in serving RAZOR CLAMS whole – with their fantastic-looking shells that look like an old cut-throat razor – but some people have an aversion to eating something that looks like it has come out of the film *Alien*. Razor clams have a wonderful sweet flavour, which is slightly peppery, I think. Large clams such as QUAHOGS (known as CHOWDERS), SURF CLAMS and GEODUCKS are best taken out of the shells (see how, page 88), sliced and used in chowders and stir-fries.

Scallops

At our restaurant, we use SMALL SCALLOPS (or QUEENS), or sometimes BAY SCALLOPS from North America, raw on the *fruits de mer*. Scallops are also great thinly sliced and served for sashimi (see page 124), where their sweetness makes a delightful contrast to the oiliness of sea trout and the texture of brill. One of our most successful dishes is grilled queenies with noisette butter (nut-brown butter) with lemon juice and parsley. You can't get much simpler than that, but I think it's the combination of nutty butter and the smell of hot shells (which I always think smell like hot beaches on a sunny day) that gets customers excited. In America, it's customary to remove the coral of scallops, which is a bit of a shame – a bit like removing the yolk from eggs. Not only are the corals lovely to eat but they can also be used to thicken sauces, just like an egg yolk.

Oysters

To me, the perfect-sized oyster is what we in Britain call a number 3 – not too big and not too small, weighing about 90g. There's a big price premium for the larger oysters (number 2s or 1s). In Europe we have two types of oyster, the NATIVE OYSTER, *Ostrea edulis*, and the PACIFIC OYSTER, *Crassostrea gigas*. The native oyster is considered the best: the most famous and revered beds are Colchester, Whitstable and Helford in England; Galway and Cork in Ireland; Belon and Arachon in France; Ostend in Belgium; Zeeland in Holland, and Limfjord in Denmark.

PACIFIC OYSTERS are much cheaper because they grow faster. They are the variety favoured for farming and crop up everywhere – favourites of mine are from Loch Fyne in Scotland and Fowey in Cornwall. The PORTUGUESE OYSTER, once considered a separate species, is now acknowledged to be the same as the Pacific. It just got to Portugal a bit earlier.

In the States the native eastern EASTERN or VIRGINIA OYSTER (*Crassostrea virginica*), is larger than the European oyster and ranges from New Brunswick in Canada right down to the Gulf of Mexico. Those from the colder northern waters are held to be the best – they grow more slowly and their shells are more uniform. The most famous beds for these are at Long Island where grow such evocatively named oysters as BLUE POINTS, and Cape Cod where WELLFLEET OYSTERS come from.

In Australia and New Zealand, the most popular species of oyster are the SYDNEY ROCK (*Saccostrea glomorata*), the PACIFIC OYSTER (*Crassostrea gigas*), the FLAT OYSTER (*Ostrea angasi*) and in New Zealand, the BLUFF OYSTER (*Tiostrea chilensis*) but the EUROPEAN OYSTER (*Ostrea edulis*) has been grown in Victoria, South and Western Australia for over a hundred years. The Sydney Rocks from Merimbula, Pambula, and in particular Ewan McAsh's Clyde River, are the stars of the seafood menu at my restaurant Rick Stein's at Bannisters at Mollymook on the South Coast of New South Wales.

In NW Australia you'll find pearl meat, a by-product of the pearl oyster fishery there. The adductor muscle of the PEARL LIP OYSTER has a white, sweet and soft texture, much sought after by Perth restaurants.

Univalves

Univalves are all those molluscs that live in one shell (unlike bivalves, which live in two shells). There's the WINKLE or PERIWINKLE, which is held in much affection by serious seafood lovers. They don't have a great taste but picking out a bowl of winkles with your winkle picker and some shallot vinegar provides an enjoyable diversion along with a glass or two of Muscadet. WHELKS too are greatly enjoyed by some. I think the small ones have the best flavour. I like them boiled and served with a choice of mayonnaise or shallot vinegar or, in the English fashion, with pepper, malt vinegar and a pint of beer. I've had success by breaking open the shells, removing the meats and stir-frying them or turning them into fritters. The MUREX is another tough, whelk-like sea snail from the Mediterranean. The attractive shell is much sought after and the TOP-SHELL, known as *bodoletti*, is popular in Venice, where it is cooked in a fireproof dish with olive oil, bay leaves and salt for about 20 minutes.

LIMPETS are reasonable eating in the same way as abalone if slow-cooked. They must have been very popular in the long past; the house I lived in on Trevose Head seems to have been built on a midden of them. There's also a univalve called the SLIPPER LIMPET, which has become a bit of a pest in Britain. It came originally from America (probably on the keel of a ship), and has since invaded a number of oyster beds, where they smother the oysters in their fight for food. But they're actually good to eat when steamed with a bit of white wine, stuffed like snails with garlic butter, and briefly grilled.

Deal with CONCH, which are found in the waters off the Florida Keys and the Caribbean, in the same way I've described for whelks, either stir-frying them or using them in fritters.

Abalone

By far the most sought-after univalve is the ABALONE (or PAUA as it's known in New Zealand, ORMER in the Channel Islands, and ORMEAU in France). But it is in the Pacific that abalone are most prolific. There are three ways of dealing with the toughness of the abalone. Slice it very thinly when raw and drop it into hot stock as the Chinese do. Bash it for a minute or so with a mallet and then fry it (for example, in breadcrumbs) or slow-cook it with oil and aromatics in a low oven for 2–3 hours. It has a similar flavour and texture to cuttlefish or octopus. The BAILER SHELL from Australia and New Zealand, sought after for its ornamental shell, is now gaining in popularity for its meat as well, which is used in the same way as abalone.

SMALL FRY

Here I've grouped together those immature fish that are caught for cooking and eating whole, but I've also included a few tiny adult fish too.

Whitebait

The general term for tiny frying fish in English is WHITEBAIT, which can actually be the fry of any number of species – although they tend to be those oily members of the herring family. In Tasmania and New Zealand they are normally tiny trout, while in the Indian Ocean a similar harvest of tiny fish is called INDIAN BAIT. In the West Indies they're PISQUETTES and on the French Mediterranean coast, NONNATS.

Sprats, blennies, capelins, gobies,
sand eels, silversides and sand smelts
These small fish are excellent cooked simply floured and deep-fried, made into fritters, or skewered, grilled and sprinkled with chopped herbs as for the recipe for sardines on page 210. SAND EELS in particular are good when floured and deep-fried. The larger ones though, known locally as LANCES, need gutting, weigh 50g or more and are better cooked like sprats. It's a matter of taste whether you remove the guts in small fish, which is a laborious procedure with something like a sprat or anchovy. A lot will depend on the cleanliness of the water in which they were caught.

THIN-BODIED FISH
Nothing in the naming of fish is perfect and a family containing a number of thin-bodied fish is clearly not a collection of related species, but rather a group selected by appearance and similar cooking qualities. Round fish have an eye on each side of their head, i.e. on each flank, while flatfish have both eyes on their top flank. The fish I've described here as flat round fish have very thin but deep bodies. Their design is perfect for concealment, whether for predatory reasons or defence, since they become almost invisible when seen head on.

John Dory
The fish that embodies this shape is the JOHN DORY, which is found in both the Atlantic and the Pacific, as far south as New Zealand. Some people refer to this lugubrious-looking, big-jawed fish as ugly, but I regard it as splendid with its expressive face, fierce eyes and astonishing array of long fins.

It's also a great fish to cook, having very firm dense white fillets with a good fresh flavour, ideal for pan-frying, grilling and chargrilling whole. It also takes a classic French cream sauce. (See the recipe on page 154.)

Pomfret
Perhaps even better known worldwide than the John Dory is the WHITE POMFRET, which is part of a small family of thin-bodied fish, which also includes RAY'S BREAM and BUTTERFISH. These are all very good eating. The pomfret is becoming increasingly popular in the UK. The fillets are close-textured and white and it's great stuffed with a masala paste, like that on page 166, and grilled. Ray's Bream is of a very fine quality too; the fish is tinged with pink and formed of long strands, rather like skate.

Opah or moonfish
Mention must be made of the OPAH or MOONFISH, a giant, thin-bodied fish which can reach 25kg. I bought some once in Woy Woy in Australia, took it back to where I was staying and pan-fried the fillets with a lick of olive oil. The flesh was pink and firm. I ate it slightly undercooked and I could have sworn I was eating scallops, it was that good. Opah, *Lampris guttatus*, can be found in both the Pacific and the Atlantic but should not be confused with the SUNFISH, which is sometimes also called moonfish, or MOLA MOLA. The sunfish is a thick-skinned, thin, gelatinous-fleshed fish found flopping around on the surface of the seas around Cornwall in the summer months and often gaffed by lobster fisherman and dragged aboard. It's of no culinary value and so much better left where it is, in the sea.

Leatherjacket and trigger-fish
These two fish, the LEATHERJACKET from Australia and New Zealand and the TRIGGER FISH from the Atlantic, closely resemble the John Dory. They have thick, leather-like skins and sharp spines just behind the eyes. Both are sold as skinned fillets and have firm flesh like that of John Dory. Trigger-fish are quite rare in Britain, normally being caught in lobster pots, but I once picked up half a dozen flapping on the beach

in Trevose where I live, flung ashore out of the surf during a winter storm.

Wrasse
Unfortunately the BALLAN WRASSE that swims off the coast of Great Britain, though of astonishingly beautiful hues of red, green and gold (and easy to catch from the rocks), is really rather tasteless. As always with fish such as this, it's good for fish soup or fish stews. However, across the world, there are much better flavoured members of this family *Labridae*.

In the USA the TAUTOG, HOGFISH, CUNNER and CALIFORNIA SHEEPHEAD are much better eating, particularly the tautog, which has very firm white meat and is especially suitable for chowders and fish stews because it doesn't break up during cooking. The California sheephead feeds on lobster and abalone and therefore has a good flavour.

Parrotfish, Maori wrasse and pigfish
Closely related to the wrasse are the PARROTFISH of the Indian Ocean, which resemble the birds in both colour and shape. They appear to have a beak and their teeth are configured somewhat like a parrot's beak in order to crush coral from which they filter out the algae they eat. If you've ever been diving on a coral reef, the sound that fills your ears underwater might well be that of grazing parrotfish. They are extremely highly regarded with firm, white and delicate-tasting flesh. The parrotfish is also present in Australian waters, along with a number of other wrasse, in particular the MAORI WRASSE, much favoured by the Chinese for inclusion in the live fish tanks of their restaurants. (Have you ever noticed the fish swim to the back of the tank as the chef approaches?) There is also the PIGFISH, which has firm, white flaky flesh and is in great demand by the Asian community. Prices for pigfish in Sydney are amongst the highest for any Australian fish.

SEA CATFISH
1. Wolf Fish
Anarhichas lupus

DEEP-SEA FISH
2. Orange Roughy
Hoplostethus atlanticus

PUFFERS
3. Northern Puffer
Sphoeroides maculatus

**MACKEREL
AND TUNA**
4. Narrow-barred
Spanish Mackerel
Scomberomorus commerson
5. Spanish Mackerel
Scomberomorus maculatus
6. Mackerel
Scomber scombrus
7. Atlantic Bonito
Sarda sarda
8. Bluefin Tuna
Thunnus thynnus

BILLFISH
9. Swordfish
Xiphias gladius

OZ CATCHALL
10. Blue-eye Trevalla
Hyperoglyphe antarctica
11. Sand Whiting
Sillago ciliata

USA CATCHALL
12. Tilefish
*Lopholatilus
chamaeleonticeps*

THIN-BODIED FISH
13. John Dory
Zeus faber
14. White Pomfret
Pampus argenteus
15. Velvet Leatherjacket
Parika scaber

FLAT FISH
16. Lemon Sole
Microstomus kitt
17. Turbot
Psetta maxima
18. Plaice
Pleuronectes platessa
19. Halibut
Hippoglossus hippoglossus
20a. Dab (underside)
20b. and 20c. Dab (top)
Limanda limanda
21. Starry Flounder
Platichthys stellatus
22. Dover Sole
Solea solea
23. Brill
Scophthalmus rhombus

ACKNOWLEDGEMENTS

I would like to thank James Murphy for all the photography and Alex Smith for the refreshing design of the book. Aya Nishimura has produced some very exciting new food styling and thanks to Debbie Major for the same from my earlier books. Once again thanks to Charlotte Knox for the wonderful fish illustrations, which originally appeared in the book *Seafood*. Commissioning editor, Lizzy Gray, and editor, Kate Fox at Ebury Books have been a pleasure to work with, as has Mari Roberts who corrected all my copy. I'd like to thank a few people at The Seafood Restaurant, my son Jack for contributing some of his recipes, my PA Viv Taylor for pulling everything together and Keith Brooksbank for testing many of the new recipes. And finally thanks to my wife, Sas, for her encouraging remarks when tasting all those new recipe ideas.